FREEDOM
AND
PROTECTION
THE
BILL
OF
RIGHTS

Let reverence for the laws be breathed by every American mother to the lisping babe that prattles on her lap; let it be taught in schools, in seminaries, and in colleges; let it be written in primers, spellingbooks, and in almanacs; let it be preached from the pulpit, proclaimed in legislative halls, and enforced in courts of justice. And, in short, let it become the political religion of the nation; and let the old and the young, the rich and the poor, the grave and the gay of all sexes and tongues and colors and conditions, sacrifice unceasingly upon its altars.

—A. LINCOLN

FREEDOM AND PROTECTION THE BILL OF RIGHTS

by

Andrew D. Weinberger

CHANDLER

PUBLISHING

COMPANY

San Francisco

FOREWORD: *PERSONAL LIBERTY IN TODAY'S WORLD*

The freedom of the people in most of the Western countries, with their alert citizenry, is reasonably assured, but in much of the world there is no liberty, and in many areas there seems to be little interest in acquiring political freedom. This indifference is in contrast to the struggles of the eighteenth and nineteenth century revolutionists in North America, in France, and in the Latin American countries. And in some countries there has been a backward movement: prior existing liberties have been surrendered in Franco's Spain and in Salazar's Portugal; in Mussolini's Italy and in Hitler's Germany they were suppressed in the 1930's. The state has been aggrandized at the expense of personal liberty under Naziism, Fascism and Russian Communism alike.

This totalitarianism is a manifestation of the materialism that, with the advent of the industrial revolution, became a driving force in the philosophy of men and nations. To say this is not to censure the rightful demand of the masses of the exploited people of the world for a fair share of the world's goods; for proper food, shelter, medical care, and education; and for participation in a cultural life and for a life without undue fears. These aspirations do not conflict with human liberty, since they cannot be achieved without first or collaterally establishing man as an individual of dignity, with the basic freedoms secure. Slavery is degradation even if the slave lives in luxury: this is the American philosophy, expressed with simple passion by Patrick Henry when he cried in the Virginia House of Burgesses, "Give me liberty or give me death."

The materialistic concept, unfortunately, is not solely the

possession of the totalitarians. It has made its inroads in the democracies. Technology and the acquisition of worldly goods, no less in America than elsewhere in the world, are now driving forces. Human freedom often loses to materialism.

A more recent and immediate danger to personal liberty stems from the fear of the state for its security. The state must and should protect itself, but it should not, out of unjustified fears and panic, destroy individual liberty. The legislative branch of the United States Government has committed a number of such excesses in recent years, but the Supreme Court generally has been a restraining influence in defending the constitutional rights of the people. The reconciliation of liberty and security is discussed in Part II of this book.

Robert H. Jackson, a Justice of the Supreme Court of the United States for the thirteen years preceding his death in 1954, and the chief United States prosecutor at the Nuremberg trials, addressing the lawyers of the French Ministry of Justice in 1946 when they were drafting a new constitution for the Fourth Republic, said:

> The legal profession in all countries knows that there are only two real choices of government open to a people. It may be governed by law or it may be governed by the will of one or of a group of men. Law, as the expression of the ultimate will and wisdom of a people, has so far proven the safest guardian of liberty yet devised. I think our constitutional and judicial system has made a valuable and enduring contribution to the science of government under law. We commend it to your notice, not because we think it is perfect, but because it is an earnest effort to fulfill those aspirations for freedom and the general welfare which are a common heritage of your people and of mine. [Jackson, *The Supreme Court in the American System of Government*, Harvard University Press (Cambridge, 1955).]

France appears not to have found it easy to govern itself within the framework of Jackson's advice. In October 1958, by a four-to-one vote, she scrapped that constitution and created the Fifth Republic in which authoritarianism and democracy, it is hoped, will be compatible. The parliament's legislative powers are limited, law may be promulgated by presidential decree, the president is also head of the judiciary and may dissolve the assembly. Whether the historic French passion for liberty will hold in check this broad assignment of powers to the president, history will tell.

Japan, with a culture in which the nation and family was all and the individual was entirely without worth, reappraised itself following the end of World War II. Its new Constitution, adopted in 1946 and effective in 1947, in its Chapter III, "Rights and Duties of the People," guarantees freedoms and protections similar to the Bill of Rights. In fact, it goes further, as it was written in a later period—it also refers to socio-economic and cultural rights.

Much of the world is in flux. One by one the former African and Asian colonies, governed since World War II under United Nations mandates, are securing their political freedom. But it is still to be seen whether national political freedom will mean personal freedom in the new republics. The martyrlike leader of the colonial revolt may become a dictator when he comes to power. The preservation of freedom is the problem of all of the people. Eternal vigilance is still the price of liberty.

CONTENTS

Part
One

THE BILL OF RIGHTS
IN HISTORY

■ ■

I

WHAT IS THE BILL OF RIGHTS?

The Constitution of the United States is the world's oldest charter of government. It was ratified in 1789, and the ten amendments which made up the Bill of Rights became effective two years later. Since then the United States has gone from an agricultural economy through the industrial revolution and has entered the space age. It has been the function of the United States Supreme Court through those years to interpret the Constitution to meet the needs of this changing society. And to do so it has from time to time reversed its own earlier constitutional interpretations—we shall see examples of such reversals in the discussion of unlawful search and of racial discrimination in schools and transportation.

Commonly, the Bill of Rights is understood to mean the first ten Articles of Amendment to the Constitution. In this book it means more: there are included in it four subsequent Amendments and several clauses from the original Constitution. The texts of these clauses and amendments are grouped in Appendix A.

The First Amendment guarantees freedom of speech, press, and religion and the right of the people peaceably to assemble and to petition the government. The Fourth Amendment prohibits unreasonable search of the home or person. The Fifth and Sixth give to the people protection of basic rights in criminal matters: an accused person may not be required to testify against himself, must be informed of the nature and cause of the accusation, may not be tried twice for the same offense, and is entitled to have a speedy and public trial by jury, to have counsel, and to be confronted by witnesses. The Fifth Amendment also prescribes that life, liberty, or property shall not be taken without due process of law. The Eighth Amendment prohibits excessive bail, and cruel and unusual punishment. The Ninth and the Tenth Amendments reserve to the States and the people all powers and liberties not enumerated in the Constitution.

The Second, Third, and Seventh Amendments are seemingly of no concern today; they relate to the quartering of troops, the right to bear arms, and the right to a jury in common-law actions for $20 or more.

The Constitution itself was adopted thirteen years after the Declaration of Independence was signed on July 4, 1776. At the Convention which drafted the Constitution for submission to the thirteen States for ratification, there was a great difference of opinion as to whether the basic rights and liberties of the people should be spelled out. Alexander Hamilton and James Madison, along with Washington, accepted the fears of James Wilson that the enumeration in the Constitution of the rights of the individual would limit liberty to what was expressly set forth and be deemed a denial of any rights that were overlooked. Thomas Jefferson forcefully took the contrary position. His opinion ultimately prevailed, though not at the Convention itself, which he did not attend. Several of the States, before ratifying the Constitution, stipulated that it be immediately amended by the inclusion of what now is the first ten Amendments and is called the Bill of Rights. These are ten of the twelve Amendments proposed to the States by the First Congress in 1789.

Other safeguards had been written into the original Constitution: Article I preserves the writ of habeas corpus (the right to a judicial determination of the legality of one's detention or imprisonment), and prohibits bills of attainder (the infliction of penalties and punishments by proceedings such as an act of Congress without a judicial hearing), and ex post facto laws (the application of a newly adopted criminal statute to conduct that was lawful when it took place); Article III limits the definition of treason to "levying War" against the United States or "adhering to their Enemies" and it requires all trials for crimes to be by jury; Article IV guarantees to the citizens of any State all the privileges of the citizens of any other State; Article VI proscribes any religious test for public office.

Immediately after the Civil War, the Thirteenth Amendment was adopted abolishing human slavery. In 1868, three years later, the Fourteenth Amendment was adopted. It requires the States to extend due process of law and equal protection of the laws to all persons, and prohibits abridgment by the States of citizens' privileges and immunities. The Fifteenth Amendment protects the right to vote against denial or abridgment because of race, color, or previous condition of servitude. No further addition to the Bill of Rights was made until 1920 when, by the Nineteenth Amendment, women were given the right of suffrage.

II

SOURCES, ANTICIPATIONS, AND CONTRASTS

Were the rights and liberties in the Constitution and its Amendments created by these documents or did these writings merely confirm rights which man has inherently?

Many people believe that these are natural rights of man, though they variously believe that they came by divine intervention, that they grew from an organized nature or physical world, or that they started with man's introspection about his place, privileges, and responsibilities in his nascent-literate culture and developed empirically, as the centuries went by, with many samenesses but some differences also, under the impact of different cultures.

The Declaration of Independence says that personal liberty comes from the "Laws of Nature" and "Nature's God" and "that all men are created equal, that they are endowed by their Creator with certain unalienable Rights, that among these are Life, Liberty, and the pursuit of Happiness." [The text of the Declaration of Independence is in Appendix B.]

Aristotle, in his *Ethics,* wrote, "Of political justice part is natural, part legal—natural, that which everywhere has the same force and does not exist by people's thinking this or that; legal, that which was originally of indifference . . . such as, that a prisoner's ransom shall be a mina, or that a goat and not two sheep shall be sacrificed."

Cicero in *De Republica* said: "True law is right reason, it is harmonious with nature, of universal application, unchanging and everlasting; it calls to duty by its commands and restrains from evil by its prohibitions. . . . It is a sacred obligation not to attempt to legislate in contradiction to this law. . . . Indeed by neither the Senate nor the people can we be released from this law. . . . Nor is it one law at Rome and another at Athens; one now and another in the future; but one eternal and unchangeable law binding all nations through all time."

And in *De Legibus,* he said: "We are born for justice, and right is not the mere arbitrary construction of opinion, but an institution of nature. Law is a rule of distinction between right and wrong according to nature, and any other sort of law ought not to be regarded as law."

There was state-law, some of it of the "other sort," as far back as 2600 B.C. From about 2000 B.C. we have Hammurabi's Code, which is historically important, though its contribution to society is only that some certainty resulted from codification. There was not one word of morality in the law of earlier Babylonian kings or of Hammurabi. The Code provided the death penalty for a multitude of offenses ranging from murder to trespass. Yet the murder of a slave was punishable only by the payment to the master of the slave's monetary value. Inferentially, a master was permitted to kill his own slave. A substantial part of the population was slaves, even slaves could own slaves, and a husband could indenture his wife and children for his debts. The Code included laws regulating commerce, the inheritance, leasing and sale of land and slaves. But it included nothing concerning any right or liberty for the vast bulk of the people who were either slaves or vassals.

The Scriptures, in Exodus 20–23, set out the moral code which is a great contribution of the Jews to civilization. In addition to initiating the concepts of the brotherhood of man and the fatherhood of God, it is a code of law that includes references to personal freedoms. It established a rule of law of individual responsibility to the state in place of the family liability or blood feuds of earlier cultures.

The Judeo-Christian ethic, basic law in Western civilization, is stated in the Ten Commandments and in other Scriptural law. Of particular significance is the injunction, "Thou shalt love thy neighbor as thyself," which first appears in Leviticus 19:18, again in Matthew 22:39, Luke 10:27, and in Chapter 13 of Paul's Epistle to the Romans. Likewise significant is the command, "The stranger that dwelleth with you shall be as one born among you and thou shalt love him as thyself" (Leviticus 19:34), which is to be found in the law of modern states that gives equal protection of the laws to all.

The Founding Fathers acknowledged their indebtedness to the Scriptures when upon the Liberty Bell, America's symbol of freedom, they had engraved, "Proclaim Liberty throughout all the land unto all the inhabitants thereof," which was taken literally from Leviticus, chapter 25. The Massachusetts colony's famous Bodye of Liberties was contemporaneously described as based upon "Moses his Judicialls."

So, the ancient Hebrews, Aristotle, and Cicero, alike ascribed the source of law elsewhere than in statute, in proclamation of the prince, or in the act of any man or men. They variously found its source and authority in God, in pagan gods, or in the rules of nature, but they unanimously maintained that certain rights existed without regard to the opinions or acts of the legislature, of the prince, or even of the majority of the population. They were in agreement that these rights had no human origin, that they were immutable and eternal.

Thomas Paine, in *Common Sense,* published before the Declaration of Independence, was pleading for such a pure morality based on natural religion when he said, ". . . let it be brought forth placed in the divine law, the word of God . . . that in America the law is King." And of this short treatise Washington said it "worked a powerful change on the minds of many men."

This concept of rights that are inherent, though not necessarily God-given, was at issue when Jefferson argued for the enumeration of individual rights in the Constitution. The Ninth Amendment, which reads, "The enumeration in the Constitution, of certain rights, shall not be construed to deny or disparage others retained by the people," is an explicit acknowledgment that there are personal liberties whether or not they are written.

The *Jus Naturale* of Cicero differed as to origin from the Decalogue, the law found in Leviticus, and the Divine Law of St. Thomas Aquinas, the thirteenth-century scholastic philosopher. Cicero looked to the Roman gods, Moses and St. Thomas to a single God, but each believed that there was a fundamental law of right and wrong established by divine guidance and that neither prince nor legislature could enact law contrary to it. Yet St. Thomas, while condemning tyranny in harsh terms, urged subjects to submit to the prince in the interests of peace and society except when the prince required a subject to commit blasphemy or sacrilege.

Much the same thinking held through the Reformation. The Protestant position was exemplified by Luther, who maintained that natural law is of divine origin and reveals injustices that may be found in statute law, but that it cannot void positive law, that is, the law adopted by a legislature or promulgated by a sovereign.

The Middle Ages, a period of princes without legislatures, called for a standard by which princes might be evaluated. One who was unduly harsh and ruled by force was contrasted with the kindly and just prince. But since he was king by divine right, what obligation was he violating? By what standard was he to be judged? Only by law from a source at least equal to the source of his own divine appointment. Hence such law as there was— that is, Roman law and the Judeo-Christian ethic—developed a stature superior to the edicts of the sovereign. If there was to be any curb upon the sovereign, any freedom under him, any protection against his arbitrary will, it had to be natural law.

In Anglo-Saxon jurisprudence, the first writing of any of these basic freedoms and protections was Magna Charta. By its terms it tells us that the barons at Runnymede in 1215, in demanding the acquiescence of King John, were asserting that he was not granting them any new rights but merely executing a covenant that he would not continue to deprive them of their God-given rights. While Magna Charta was a great step forward in the struggle for human liberty in that it limited the law-making rights of the king, it was in fact a great declaration of rights principally for the barons. In many ways it was in derogation of the rights of the people as it increased the power of the petty nobility over the serfs. Yet it was a first step, and upon it has been built the entire body of English and American guaranties of individual liberty.

More than four centuries later, a series of persistent violations of the personal liberty which was formulated in Magna Charta led to the Bill of Rights of 1689. William of Orange was brought in and crowned upon his signing the Declaration and Bill of Rights which restated the guaranteed rights of liberty and itemized the many previous violations of Magna Charta by the Crown. These two instruments are the framework around which American constitutional government has been built.

In the late seventeenth century the work of Sir Isaac Newton in physics and mathematics revived natural law as a doctrine and won for it a greater acceptance than it ever had before or since. With his exposition of the law of gravitation, Newton established in men's thinking the postulate that all nature, that is, all the physical world, is ordered and is part of one general plan. The influence of this reasoning prepared the ground for a new and fuller acceptance of natural law.

Thomas Hobbes, who wrote earlier in the seventeenth century, had many followers for his thesis that in the state of nature every man was an aggressor, that men were wolves and at each other's throats, that men started to live in society and entered into a social compact only for self-preservation, and that each surrendered his right to be a wolf in return for protection from other wolves. Hence, he argued, the prince has almost unlimited power. His view has not prevailed.

John Locke, in 1690, wrote the *Second Treatise of Civil Government* to justify the Glorious Revolution of 1688 and explain the import of the Declaration and Bill of Rights of the year 1689. In all proper states, he said, the prince and the legislature were subordinate to the basic natural law: the right to life, liberty, and property. And, said Locke, if the legislature or the prince denied these rights to the people they should revolt and set up a new government.

The impact of Locke was tremendous. His philosophy underlay the Declaration of Independence, the Constitution, and the Bill of Rights in America and the Declaration of the Rights of Man in France.

The Declaration of Independence, like the Declaration of Rights of Man, contains broad assertions of the right to freedom without any specific enumeration, that is, without any definition of the extent of the rights or of the way in which they are to be secured. The inefficacy and insufficiency of such a general exordium is shown by the fact that in the presence of chattel slavery Thomas Jefferson could write, in the Declaration of Independence, ". . . that all men are created equal, that they are endowed by their Creator with certain unalienable Rights, that among these are Life, Liberty and the pursuit of Happiness." Though the natural law of Locke and his predecessors was an intellectual instrument to restrict despotic governments, it was philosophy, at best a guide in the absence of statutory law, for a court with a problem to adjudicate. Likewise, the Declaration of the Rights of Man, the Declaration of Independence, and in our generation the Universal Declaration of Human Rights, though among man's greatest instruments, are merely exordial. They contain no process of enforcement. [The text of the Universal Declaration of Human Rights, with a commentary, is in Appendix D.]

Similarly, the unwritten constitution of England and the written constitutions of France, other European countries, and the Latin American republics are not law which binds legislatures. They are declarations of policy, and legislation contrary to their tenets is valid.

A more direct instrument has come into force in Canada. The Canadian Parliament, in August 1960, unanimously passed "An Act for the Recognition and Protection of Human Rights and Fundamental Freedoms." While its purpose is to insure personal freedom for the future, the Act is not a legal restriction on future legislators as is the United States Constitution. However, it is substantially more than most other constitutions, which are scarcely more than exhortations. The Act provides that every law of Canada shall be so construed and applied as "not to abrogate, abridge or infringe" on any of the freedoms in the Canadian Bill of Rights unless it is expressly declared by Parliament that "it shall operate notwithstanding the Canadian Bill of Rights." [The text of the Canadian Bill of Rights is in Appendix C.]

The Bill of Rights in the Constitution of the United

States (and also the Japanese Constitution of 1946, and the Philippine Constitution of 1935), by contrast to other constitutions, is not merely a group of maxims of political morality or advice to future legislators. It is a set of restrictions coupled with sanctions: it is "the supreme Law of the Land."

III

JUDICIAL REVIEW

The interpreting of the Constitution by the Supreme Court is called judicial review. The Constitution established the Supreme Court but did not expressly assign to it this function of judicial review. The Court, however, soon found it necessary to assume the right to test the validity of the acts of the Congress and of the executive branch of the government against the liberties reserved by the people in the Constitution. Since 1803 it has performed this task, often against the outcry of Congresses, Presidents, and large segments of the population.

But from where came this right of judicial review? It is not to be found in express words in either the original Constitution or the Amendments. Neither may it be found in English jurisprudence. It was four centuries after the signing of Magna Charta when an English court in *Bonham's case* for the first time asserted the privilege to hold a law invalid as violative of the constitution. England had no written constitution then and has none now. The reference to the English constitution is to the unwritten English common law, which is to be found in custom and in the decisions of the courts. When Sir Edward Coke in 1610 had *Bonham's case* for adjudication, there was no precedent. The King had granted to the members of the London College of Physicians the exclusive right to practice medicine in that city. Dr. Bonham was charged with practicing medicine illegally because he was not a member of the London College. Coke, noted for his arrogance though his friends called it courage, held the King's charter void as in violation of the common law. In doing so he set a landmark in jurisprudence as well as a new standard for the independence and integrity of the judiciary. He said: "When an Act of Parliament is against common right and reason, or repugnant, or impossible to be performed, the common law will control it and adjudge such Act to be void." With this decision, in which the reference to Parliament was only dictum (a statement of law, in a judicial opinion, not required for determination of the case), Coke declared the doctrine of judicial review: the right of a court to say that an order of the prince, or an act of the legislature, is invalid and not law if it violates rights reserved in the constitution.

This doctrine was promptly repudiated in England—the English courts may not test acts of Parliament or the sovereign against what is called the English constitution. But historically *Dr. Bonham's case* is important as it was the occasion for the first judicial statement of the political concept under which our courts validate and invalidate acts of the President as well as those of Congress within the ambit of the Constitution.

The Constitution sets out a form of government consisting of three branches: the legislative, the executive, and the judicial, each independent of the other. If one branch could set aside the acts of another, as, for example, a court invalidate an act of the legislature, then where was the postulate of three independent departments of government? Yet, what would the situation be if one were to deny to the courts the right to determine the constitutionality of the law?

Concededly, the Constitution is the supreme law of the land. Article VI says: "This Constitution . . . and all Treaties . . . shall be the supreme Law of the Land . . .".

There is a general principle that when a law is in conflict with an earlier one, even in the absence of special reference, the later law repeals or supersedes the earlier. It would seem, then, that an act of Congress in conflict with the Constitution would prevail and be a modification of the Constitution. It could do so, however, only if the act and the Constitution were of equal validity or origin. The Constitution is the fundamental law adopted by the people, and the legislature, though elected by them, is not the same thing as the people. The conflict between constitutional law, the law of the people, and a law made by a representative legislature must be resolved in favor of the Constitution.

But who shall make the decision as to whether or not there is a constitutional conflict? The legislature expressed its opinion in adopting the questioned law. We may assume that the legislators would not have passed the statute if they considered it unconstitutional.

Shall the executive branch of the government then make the determination? Hardly, for that would to all effects and purposes create a tyranny, giving the executive, in such a situation, the right to make his own determination as to whether he chose to enforce any act of the legislature.

But why the courts? If the power of determining constitutionality is theirs, does not that power make them the paramount rulers of the country? Perhaps to some extent it does, but ultimate resolution must be made by one branch or other of the government, and it is the usual and ordinary function of a court to interpret and determine the law, its meaning, and its extent. From this reasoning it follows that when there is conflict between an act of Congress and the Constitution, the courts are to test the legislative act against the constitutional limitations. Even so, the final decision rests with the people. When an act of Congress or of the executive department is overruled by the Supreme Court as violative of constitutional protection, the Congress may, within the ambit of the constitution, enact a new statute, or the people may, as provided in the Constitution, amend it so that the rejected law may then be adopted anew without any infirmity.

This right of review did not come to the courts without debate. Jefferson thought each branch of the government was to make its own determination and that it was not accountable or responsible to any other department of the government. He said that one who received delegated powers was responsible only to the grantor of the powers or to a higher authority. As an academic statement, that is correct, but were one to apply it as an organizing principle of government, it would create anarchy. (Jefferson, despite his strong feelings about separation of powers, once wrote, "In the arguments . . . one . . . has great weight with me, the legal check which it puts into the hands of the Judiciary.")

No government could endure as a democracy wherein the legislature could pass any law it chose if in its sole judgment it did not violate the Constitution, and wherein, when it became necessary to execute or enforce the law, the executive branch of the government could decide for itself that the law was unconstitutional and refuse to enforce it. That arrangement would relegate the legislature to a mere advisory position.

The people adopted the Constitution and delegated lawmaking powers to Congress. As they declared the Constitution the supreme law of the land, it follows that the powers they gave to Congress are limited by the Constitution. The people, being the grantor of the powers of Congress, they may declare invalid acts of Congress which violate Constitutional limitations. This is a collective right of the entire body politic exercised for the people by the courts.

Alexander Hamilton stated the case for judicial review in Number 78 of *The Federalist,* where he wrote:

> It is far more rational to suppose that the courts were designed to be be an intermediate body between the people and the legislature in order among other things to keep the latter within the limits assigned to their authority. The interpretation of the laws is the proper and peculiar province of the courts. A constitution is, in fact, and must be regarded by the judges, as a fundamental law . . . where the will of the legislature declared in its statutes stands in opposition to that of the people declared by the Constitution, the judges ought to be governed by the latter rather than the former.

The debate was continuous from the Constitutional Convention until the decision of the Supreme Court in *Marbury v. Madison* in 1803, in which it was established that the United States Supreme Court passes on the constitutionality of legislative acts. But the complaints against judicial review, reasonably quiescent for over a century, were heard anew in the days of the 1930 New Deal legislation and have been particularly violent since the Court's decisions of the last few years in the *School Segregation Cases* and in security matters. In *Marbury,* Chief Justice Marshall said:

It is, emphatically, the province and duty of the judicial department, to say what the law is. Those who apply the rule to particular cases, must of necessity expound and interpret that rule. If two laws conflict with each other, the courts must decide on the operation of each. So, if a law be in opposition to the constitution; if both the law and the constitution apply to a particular case, so that the court must either decide that case, comformable to the law, disregarding the constitution; or comformable to the constitution, disregarding the law; the court must determine which of these conflicting rules governs the case: this is of the very essence of judicial duty. If then, the courts are to regard the constitution, and the constitution is superior to any ordinary act of the legislature, the constitution, and not such ordinary act, must govern the case to which they both apply. [*Marbury v. Madison,* 5 U.S. 137 (1803)]

The doctrine of judicial review is now the law of the land. Constitutional decisions of recent years have not been concerned with whether the courts have the right of review, but with deciding how constitutional liberties enunciated in the eighteenth century are to be applied in twentieth-century America.

The Court's record in earlier years is in sharp contrast to many of the holdings of the present Court. In 1857, in the "history-making" Dred Scott decision [*Scott v. Sanford,* 19 How. 393], the Court held that a Negro had ". . . no rights which a white man was bound to respect." This ruling gave the highest legal sanction to the dehumanization of the colored race, and was an important factor in hastening the Civil War.

After the Civil War, during the Reconstruction Period, the Court repeatedly held that state-imposed racial segregation was discrimination *per se* and accordingly a violation of the equal protection clause of the Fourteenth Amendment. [*Strauder v. West Virginia;* the Court's opinion, in abridgment, is at page 36.]

But in 1896, the Court, in one decision [*Plessy v. Ferguson,* 163 U.S. 537], destroyed nearly all that had been achieved constitutionally for civil rights by giving legal sanction to the "separate but equal" doctrine which validated segregation legislation, provided "equal" facilities or services were made available to colored persons. This doctrine was the law for more than half a century.

In the beginning of this century and the preceding decade,

the Court was dedicated to the doctrine that private property rights were the beginning and end of Constitutional rights, forgetting that the framers of the Constitution had been primarily concerned with the personal freedoms.

But in recent years the Court in case after case has held that citizens are individuals of worth and dignity. The Court has not only maintained democracy as such but specifically it has preserved the freedoms of minorities which could be lawfully violated in a democracy if the legislature, elected and governed by majority rule, were not limited by a fundamental law such as the Bill of Rights.

Part
Two

THE BILL OF RIGHTS TODAY

■ ■

IV

RELIGIOUS LIBERTY

Many of the early American settlers came to the English colonies seeking liberty to practice their religion. But some sectarians, when they found themselves in power, were intolerant of religions other than their own. Victims of bigotry though they had been before emigrating to the New World, many of the colonists were not ready to extend religious liberty to others.

But from the conflict in interest of different controlling sects, in the thirteen former colonies that wished to federate, came constitutional guarantees of freedom of religion. And in the interval between the Revolution and the adoption of the Constitution, Virginia, in 1786, after a seven-year bitter struggle led by Jefferson and Madison, passed the Bill for Establishing Religious Freedom granting complete religious liberty. The Virginia Bill is the first known law of its kind anywhere; it was the base on which were founded the subsequent constitutional safeguards of religious freedom. They in turn have exercised an influence throughout the world.

The forthright language of the Virginia preamble includes the statements:

> that . . . to suffer the civil magistrate to intrude his powers into the field of opinion . . . is a dangerous fallacy, which at once destroys all religious liberty, because he . . . will make his opinions the rule of judgment, and approve or condemn the sentiments of others only as they shall square with or differ from his own; that it is time enough for the rightful purposes of civil government, for its officers to interfere, when principles break out into overt acts against peace and good order; and finally, that truth is great and will prevail, if left to herself; that she is the proper and sufficient antagonist to error, and has nothing to fear from the conflict.

The statutory grants and prohibitions were no less forceful:

> . . . no man shall be compelled to frequent or support any re-
> ligious worship, place or ministry whatsoever, nor shall be en-
> forced, restrained, molested, or burthened in his body or goods. . . .
> all men shall be free to profess, and by argument to maintain, their
> opinions in matters of religion, and that the same shall be in no
> wise diminish, enlarge or affect their civil capacities.

The Constitution, as adopted in 1789, contains no provision
as to religion except the prohibition in Article VI that ". . . no
religious Test shall ever be required as a Qualification to any
Office or public Trust under the United States."

The Bill of Rights, adopted two years later, has in the
First Amendment a prohibition against Congress's establishing
a state religion or interfering with anyone's exercise of any religion. The language is explicit and the guaranty of freedom
of belief is absolute. But even though the Amendment seems to
protect anything one does as a religious observance, inhibitions
have nevertheless, over the years, been placed on action as differ-
entiated from belief. While there have been other conflicts between religious freedom and public policy, the two most note-
worthy have concerned (a) the Quakers and others who refuse
to bear arms, and (b) the Mormons who in the nineteenth century not only permitted but even required polygamous marriage.

The Quakers and other well-established sects have been
upheld in their right to their religious convictions, whereas the
Mormons have not been allowed to practice polygamy. When
the Mormons asserted in court that the penal prohibition of
polygamy violated their constitutional religious rights, the United
States Supreme Court held that though freedom of belief is
without limitation one may not in the name of religious observance violate criminal statutes [*Reynolds v. U.S.*, 98 U.S. 145
(1878)]. Otherwise, in the name of religion, any and all law
could be reversed.

Yet under the doctrine of religious freedom, both in World
War I and World War II, those who were members of organized
religions which prohibited military service were excused from
bearing arms. This exemption was accomplished by special leg-

islation. The Constitution undoubtedly was its inspiration, but the First Amendment by itself would not have relieved these persons from military service. Conscientious objectors did not have an easy time—there were many cases of extreme hardship— but the law recognized their moral conflict.

In summary, the right of freedom of religious belief is absolute, but conduct prescribed or allowed by one's religion must conform to the penal and other laws of society.

A concomitant of the individual's right of religious freedom is the First Amendment prohibition against Congress's establishing a state religion. Although there has been no attempt by any church to become a national religious establishment, there have been many attempts, some of which have been successful, to partially break down the separation of church and state.

The holdings of the Supreme Court have been that State action encouraging religious activity is permissible provided the aid is not sectarian. Illinois provided for voluntary religious instruction of thirty to forty-five minutes a week by separating the children into groups who were to continue with their regular school work, and others who were to meet in groups of their own sects. Each of these latter groups was instructed by a religious leader of its own denomination. Despite the voluntary nature of the procedure, the Court held it violative of the Constitution, as the instruction was in the school building. [*McCollum v. Board of Education;* the Court's opinion, in abridgment, is at page 25.] But four years later, in 1952, the Court upheld the New York law which permitted for such students as requested it release from 30 minutes a week of school attendance for religious instruction outside the school. [*Zorach v. Clauson,* 343 U.S. 306] The Court has also upheld as constitutional various laws under which State money is used to benefit parochial school pupils for purposes other than religious instruction, such as the provision of textbooks and buses. [*Everson v. Board of Education;* the Court's opinion, in abridgment, is at page 27.]

All the fifty States except Alaska have laws ("blue laws") prohibiting all or some commercial activity on Sunday. Seventh Day Adventists, Orthodox Jews, and others whose Sabbath is not the first day of the week are exempted from the blue laws of twenty-one of these states. Ancient Sunday laws included an order of Henry III of England, who, in 1237, forbade marketing on Sunday and a Roman decree, posted in 321 by Constantine, requiring that all but farmers "rest on the venerable day of the Sun." Virginia, in 1610, adopted the first of the colonial blue laws. While it was enforced to a considerable extent, at no time was its provision of death for a third offense invoked. This pattern of permissive noncompliance has continued in most communities to this day. In 1961, the Court, on appeals from blue laws of Pennsylvania, Maryland, and Massachusetts, upheld the statutes holding that they did not violate the "establishment of religion" or "free exercise" of religion clauses of the First Amendment. In the principal opinion Chief Justice Warren said:

> People of all religions and people with no religion regard Sunday as a time for family activity, for visiting friends and relatives, for late-sleeping, for passive and active entertainments, for dining out and the like. . . . as presently written and administered most [blue laws] are of a secular rather than a religious character. [*McGowan v. Maryland,* and three other cases, 366 U.S. 420 (1961)]

Some fear that these encroachments on the separation of church and state may be extended and become a substantial impediment to religious freedom. But throughout these recurring controversies, the First Amendment and Article VI stand as the defenders of the freedom to choose one's own religion and, to a lesser extent, the freedom to have none at all.

McCOLLUM v. BOARD OF EDUCATION, 333 U.S. 203 (1948)

Abridgment of Mr. Justice Black's Opinion for the Court. (Mr. Justice Frankfurter concurred in a separate opinion in which Mr. Justice Jackson, Mr. Justice Rutledge, and Mr. Justice Burton joined.)

In 1940 interested members of the Jewish, Roman Catholic, and a few of the Protestant faiths formed a voluntary association called the Champaign Council on Religious Education. They obtained permission from the Board of Education to offer classes in religious instruction to public school pupils in grades four to nine inclusive. Classes were made up of pupils whose parents signed printed cards requesting that their children be permitted to attend; they were held weekly, thirty minutes for the lower grades, forty-five minutes for the higher. The council employed the religious teachers at no expense to the school authorities, but the instructors were subject to the approval and supervision of the superintendent of schools. Classes were conducted in the regular classrooms of the school building. Students who did not choose to take the religious instruction were not released from public school duties; they were required to leave their classrooms and go to some other place in the school building for pursuit of their secular studies. On the other hand, students who were released from secular study for the religious instruction were required to be present at the religious classes. Reports of their presence or absence were to be made to their secular teachers.

The foregoing facts, without reference to others that appear in the record, show the use of tax-supported property for religious instruction and the close cooperation between the school authorities and the religious council in promoting religious education. The operation of the State's compulsory education system thus assists and is integrated with the program of religious instruction carried on by separate religious sects.

To hold that a State cannot consistently with the First and Fourteenth Amendments utilize its public school system to aid any or all religious faiths or sects in the dissemination of their doctrines and ideals does not, as counsel urge, manifest a governmental hostility to religion or religious teachings. A manifestation of such hostility would be at war with our national tradition as embodied in the First Amendment's guaranty of the free exercise of religion. For the First

Amendment rests upon the premise that both religion and government can best work to achieve their lofty aims if each is left free from the other within its respective sphere. Or, as we said in the *Everson* case, the First Amendment has erected a wall between Church and State which must be kept high and impregnable.

Here not only are the State's tax-supported public school buildings used for the dissemination of religious doctrines. The State also affords sectarian groups an invaluable aid in that it helps to provide pupils for their religious classes through use of the State's compulsory public school machinery. This is not separation of Church and State.

The cause is reversed and remanded to the State Supreme Court for proceedings not inconsistent with this opinion.

EVERSON v. BOARD OF EDUCATION, 330 U.S. 1 (1947)

Abridgment of Mr. Justice Black's Opinion for the Court. (Mr. Justice Jackson dissented in an opinion in which Mr. Justice Frankfurter concurred. Mr. Justice Rutledge dissented in a separate opinion in which Mr. Justice Burton concurred.)

A New Jersey statute authorizes its local school districts to make rules and contracts for the transportation of children to and from schools. The appellee, a township board of education, acting pursuant to this statute, authorized reimbursement to parents of money expended by them for the bus transportation of their children on regular busses operated by the public transportation system. Part of this money was for the payment of transportation of some children in the community to Catholic parochial schools. These church schools give their students, in addition to secular education, regular religious instruction conforming to the religious tenets and modes of worship of the Catholic Faith. The superintendent of these schools is a Catholic priest.

The appellant, in his capacity as district taxpayer, filed suit in a state court challenging the right of the Board to reimburse parents of parochial school students. He contended that the statute and the resolution passed pursuant to it violated both the State and the Federal Constitutions. That court held that the legislature was without power to authorize such payment under the State constitution. The New Jersey Court of Errors and Appeals reversed, holding that neither the statute nor the resolution passed pursuant to it was in conflict with the State constitution or the provisions of the Federal Constitution in issue.

The only contention here is that the state statute and the resolution, insofar as they authorized reimbursement to parents of children attending parochial schools, violate the Federal Constitution in these two respects, which to some extent overlap. *First.* They authorize the State to take by taxation the private property of some and bestow it upon others, to be used for their own private purposes. This, it is alleged, violates the due process clause of the Fourteenth Amendment. *Second.* The statute and the resolution forced inhabitants to pay taxes to help support and maintain schools which are dedicated to, and which regularly teach, the Catholic Faith. This is alleged to be a use of state power to support church schools contrary to the

27

prohibition of the First Amendment which the Fourteenth Amendment made applicable to the states.

First. The due process argument that the state law taxes some people to help others carry out their private purposes is framed in two phases. The first phase is that a state cannot tax A to reimburse B for the cost of transporting his children to church schools. This is said to violate the due process clause because the children are sent to these church schools to satisfy the personal desires of their parents, rather than the public's interest in the general education of all children. But, the New Jersey legislature has decided that a public purpose will be served by using tax-raised funds to pay the bus fares of all school children, including those who attend parochial schools. The New Jersey Court of Errors and Appeals has reached the same conclusion. The fact that a state law, passed to satisfy a public need, coincides with the personal desires of the individuals most directly affected is certainly an inadequate reason for us to say that a legislature has erroneously appraised the public need.

It is much too late to argue that legislation intended to facilitate the opportunity of children to get a secular education serves no public purpose. Nor does it follow that a law has a private rather than a public purpose because it provides that tax-raised funds will be paid to reimburse individuals on account of money spent by them in a way which furthers a public program. Subsidies and loans to individuals such as farmers and home-owners, and to privately owned transportation systems, as well as many other kinds of businesses, have been commonplace practices in our state and national history.

Insofar as the second phase of the due process argument may differ from the first, it is by suggesting that taxation for transportation of children to church schools constitutes support of a religion by the State. But if the law is invalid for this reason, it is because it violates the First Amendment's prohibition against the establishment of religion by law. This is the exact question raised by appellant's second contention. . . .

Second. The New Jersey statute is challenged as a "law respecting an establishment of religion."

The meaning and scope of the First Amendment, preventing establishment of religion or prohibiting the free exercise thereof, in the light of its history and the evils it was designed forever to suppress, have been several times elaborated by the decisions of this Court prior to the application of the First Amendment to the states by the Fourteenth. The broad meaning given the Amendment by these earlier cases has been accepted by this Court in its decisions concerning an individual's religious freedom rendered since the Fourteenth Amendment was interpreted to make the prohibitions of the First applicable to state action abridging religious freedom. There is every reason to give the same application and broad interpretation to the "establishment of religion" clause. The interrelation of these complementary clauses was well summarized in a statement of the Court of Appeals of South Carolina, quoted with approval by this Court in *Watson v. Jones:* "The structure of our government has, for the preservation of civil liberty, rescued the temporal institutions from religious interference. On the other hand, it has secured religious liberty from the invasion of the civil authority."

The "establishment of religion" clause of the First Amendment means at least this: Neither a state nor the Federal Government can set up a church. Neither can pass laws which aid one religion, aid all religions, or prefer one religion over another. Neither can force nor influence a person to go to or to remain away from church against his will or force him to profess a belief or disbelief in any religion. No person can be punished for entertaining or professing religious beliefs or disbeliefs, for church attendance or non-attendance. No tax in any amount, large or small, can be levied to support any religious activities or institutions, whatever they may be called, or whatever form they may adopt to teach or practice religion. Neither a state nor the Federal Government can, openly or secretly, participate in the affairs of any religious organizations or groups and *vice versa.* In the words of Jefferson, the clause against establishment of religion by law was intended to erect "a wall of separation between church and State."

We must consider the New Jersey statute in accordance with the foregoing limitations imposed by the First Amendment. But we must not strike that state statute down if it is within the State's constitutional power even though it approaches the verge of that power. New Jersey cannot consistently with the "establishment of religion" clause of the First Amendment contribute tax-raised funds to the support of an institution which teaches the tenets and faith of any church. On the other hand, other language of the amendment commands that New Jersey cannot hamper its citizens in the free exercise of their own religion. Consequently, it cannot exclude individual Catholics, Lutherans, Mohammedans, Baptists, Jews, Methodists, Non-believers, Presbyterians, or the members of any other faith, *because of their faith, or lack of it,* from receiving the benefits of public welfare legislation. While we do not mean to intimate that a state could not provide transportation only to children attending public schools, we must be careful, in protecting the citizens of New Jersey against state-established churches, to be sure that we do not inadvertently prohibit New Jersey from extending its general state law benefits to all its citizens without regard to their religious belief.

Measured by these standards, we cannot say that the First Amendment prohibits New Jersey from spending tax-raised funds to pay the bus fares of parochial school pupils as a part of a general program under which it pays the fares of pupils attending public and other schools. It is undoubtedly true that children are helped to get to church schools. There is even a possibility that some of the children might not be sent to the church schools if the parents were compelled to pay their children's bus fares out of their own pockets when transportation to a public school would have been paid for by the State. The same possibility exists where the state requires a local transit company to provide reduced fares to school children including those attending parochial schools, or where a municipally owned transportation system undertakes to carry all school children free of charge. Moreover, state-paid policemen, detailed to protect children going to and from church schools from the very real hazards of traffic, would serve much the same purpose and accomplish much the same result as state provisions intended to guarantee free transportation of a kind which the state deems to be best for the school children's welfare. And parents might refuse to risk their children to the serious danger of traffic accidents going to and from parochial schools, the approaches to which were not protected by policemen. Similarly, parents might be reluctant to permit their children to attend schools which the state had cut off from such general government services as ordinary police and fire protection, connections for sewage disposal, public highways and sidewalks. Of course, cutting off church schools from these services, so separate and so indisputably marked off by the religious function, would make it far more difficult for the schools to operate. But such is obviously not the purpose of the First Amendment. That Amendment requires the state to be a neutral in its relations with groups of religious believers and non-believers; it does not require the state to be their adversary. State power is no more to be used so as to handicap religions than it is to favor them.

This Court has said that parents may, in the discharge of their duty under state compulsory education laws, send their children to a religious rather than a public school if the school meets the secular educational requirements which the state has power to impose. It appears that these parochial schools meet New Jersey's requirements. The State contributes no money to the schools. It does not support them. Its legislation, as applied, does no more than provide a general program to help parents get their children, regardless of their religion, safely and expeditiously to and from accredited schools.

The First Amendment has erected a wall between church and state. That wall must be kept high and impregnable. We could not approve the slightest breach. New Jersey has not breached it here.

V

PROTECTION AGAINST
RACIAL DISCRIMINATION

President Lincoln, by his Emancipation Proclamation in 1863 during the course of the Civil War, freed the slaves in areas that were in rebellion. But not until the Thirteenth Amendment was adopted in 1865 was slavery abolished throughout the country. In 1868 the Fourteenth Amendment was adopted; it requires the States to proceed by due process of law and to grant equal protection of the law to all persons without regard to color or other classification. And in 1870, the Fifteenth Amendment was adopted protecting the right to vote regardless of race, color, or previous condition of servitude.

The Fourteenth Amendment is a prohibition against acts by the States, not against acts by individuals. The South had attempted to maintain some of the conditions of slavery even though slavery itself had been abolished. Both in the South and elsewhere, social discriminations and segregation were and are practiced by white persons in their relations with colored people; State legislatures from time to time, down to the present day, have enacted laws discriminating against Negroes. Such laws are enacted even though any discrimination by a State has been declared illegal by the United States Supreme Court. In 1879, eleven years after the adoption of the Fourteenth Amendment, the Court reversed a Negro's conviction in the West Virginia courts because Negroes were by law excluded from jury panels. The Court said:

> . . . all persons, whether colored or white, shall stand equal before the laws of the States, and, in regard to the colored race, for whose protection the amendment was primarily designed, that no dis-

crimination shall be made against them by law because of their color. . . . [*Strauder v. West Virginia;* the Court's opinion, in abridgment, it at page 36.]

Discriminatory municipal ordinances are likewise illegal. Louisville, Kentucky in 1914 enacted an ordinance establishing Negro and white residential districts. When Buchanan, a Negro, found that the ordinance prohibited him from building a house on the land he had contracted to purchase, he brought an action at the end of which the United States Supreme Court held that the ordinance was invalid because it violated the Fourteenth Amendment. In this case, there was a willing seller and a willing buyer for the land. The only obstacle to Buchanan's building his house was the municipal law which the Court struck down as violative of the equal protection clause of the Fourteenth Amendment. [*Buchanan v. Warley*, 245 U.S. 60 (1917)]

Discriminatory segregation in housing was not ended, however, by the *Buchanan* decision. Two other patterns of racial housing segregation spread through the country. One was the "gentlemen's agreement," an unwritten understanding by white persons not to sell homes to Negroes in white neighborhoods. This practice is still common, though by 1961 Colorado, Connecticut, Massachusetts, Minnesota, New Hampshire, New Jersey, New York, Oregon, and Pennsylvania had laws generally prohibiting discrimination in private housing. There were similar prohibitions, but limited to various kinds of publicly assisted housing, in nine other States, and thirty-three cities had similar ordinances or resolutions.

Idaho, New Hampshire, North Dakota, and Wyoming in 1961 for the first time enacted legislation banning discrimination in places of public accommodation. These acts brought the number of States with such laws to twenty-seven. Bills to establish or strengthen civil rights in various areas were before the 1961 legislatures of 31 states. The Provincial Legislature of Ontario in 1961 adopted the first Canadian fair housing law.

The other means taken to circumvent the ruling in the *Buchanan* case was a far-flung, though not a universal, practice of community developers and property owners placing restrictions on land by a covenant that it could not be sold to or occupied by Negroes. (Some restrictive covenants included Asiatics, Mexicans, Indians, and other ethnic groups.) Land so encumbered was still restricted even though years later a new owner wanted to convey it to a colored purchaser. To enforce such a racial housing covenant, preventing a willing seller from transferring his property to a Negro purchaser, an interested party could secure an injunction from the courts. In time, after many defeats in the State courts, those who found these covenants reprehensible reached the United States Supreme Court with cases from northern and southern States and from the District of Columbia. The rationale of the cases was not that the covenants were void but that their *enforcement by a State court* was an act of discrimination by the State and was accordingly prohibited by the Fourteenth Amendment. The Court sustained this reasoning and held:

> So long as the purposes of those agreements are effectuated by voluntary adherence to their terms, it would appear clear that there has been no action by the State and the provisions of the Amendment have not been violated. . . . [But] The owners of the properties were willing sellers; and contracts of sale were accordingly consummated. It is clear that but for the active intervention of the state courts, supported by the full panoply of state power, petitioners would have been free to occupy the properties in question without restraint. [*Shelley v. Kramer*, 334 U.S. 1 (1948)]

The *Shelley* case was the death knell for racial residential land covenants. They are entirely meaningless and cannot be enforced today.

The proponents of segregation had found legal vindication in 1896 in *Plessy v. Ferguson* [163 U.S. 537], in which the United States Supreme Court upheld as lawful the separation of the races in railway transportation as long as the accommodations were equal. While the determination was only as to transportation, the rule was adopted in practice for schools and all public facilities.

This "separate but equal" doctrine was the law of the land until 1954, when, in the *School Segregation Cases* [the Court's opinion, in abridgment, is at page 39] the Supreme Court held that separation itself was a denial of equality. In 1955 the Court ordered that public schools be desegregated with all deliberate speed. Since then, in various regions, there has been violent opposition to effectuating the order of the Court. But the opposition is being fought State by State and school by school, and gradually but surely law is prevailing.

The *School Segregation Cases* were concerned only with education, but the rule they promulgated—that separation even when coupled with equality of facilities is discrimination—is now a general rule of law and not limited to schools. The Court made that general application clear in 1956, when it held that an Alabama statute requiring segregation in intrastate transportation violated the equal protection clause of the Fourteenth Amendment even though the accommodations were equal. [*Gayle v. Browder*, 352 U.S. 903 (1956)] It had been previously held that there may be no segregation in interstate transportation, as that would be the sort of undue burden on interstate commerce which is prohibited by the Constitution. [*Morgan v. Virginia*, 328 U.S. 373 (1946)] Prompted by the Freedom Riders and under the authority of the *Morgan* case, the Interstate Commerce Commission, in 1961, issued an order to all interstate bus lines that terminals, restaurants, ticket offices, and all other facilities that they use, whether or not they control them, were required to operate without any segregation.

The law of the land today is that there may be no racial discrimination or separation of the races, even with equal facilities, by a municipality, a State, or the Federal government in their own activities or by municipal ordinance or State legislation regulating privately owned public facilities.

STRAUDER v. WEST VIRGINIA,
100 U.S. 303 (1879)

Abridgment of Mr. Justice Strong's Opinion for the Court. (Mr. Chief Justice Field dissented.)

The plaintiff in error, a colored man, was indicted for murder in the Circuit Court of Ohio County, in West Virginia, on the 20th of October, 1874, and upon trial was convicted and sentenced.

The law of the State . . . is as follows: "All white male persons who are twenty-one years of age and who are citizens of this State shall be liable to serve as jurors, except as herein provided." The persons excepted are State officials.

In this court, several errors have been assigned, and the controlling questions underlying them all are, first, whether, by the Constitution and laws of the United States, every citizen of the United States has a right to a trial of an indictment against him by a jury selected and impanelled without discrimination against his race or color, because of race or color; . . .

It is to be observed that the first of these questions is not whether a colored man, when an indictment has been preferred against him, has a right to a grand or a petit jury composed in whole or in part of persons of his own race or color, but it is whether, in the composition or selection of jurors by whom he is to be indicted or tried, all persons of his race or color may be excluded by law, solely because of their race or color, so that by no possibility can any colored man sit upon the jury.

[The Fourteenth Amendment] ordains that no State shall make or enforce any laws which shall abridge the privileges or immunities of citizens of the United States (evidently referring to the newly made citizens, who, being citizens of the United States, are declared to be also citizens of the State in which they reside). It ordains that no State shall deprive any person of life, liberty, or property, without due process of law, or deny to any person within its jurisdiction the equal protection of the laws. What is this but declaring that the law in the States shall be the same for the black as for the white; that all persons, whether colored or white, shall stand equal before the laws of the States, and, in regard to the colored race, for whose protection the amendment was primarily designed, that no discrimination shall be made against them by law because of their color? The words of the amendment, it is true, are prohibitory, but they contain a necessary implication of a positive immunity, or right, most valuable to the colored race,—the right to exemption from unfriendly legislation against them distinctively as colored,—exemption from legal discriminations, implying inferiority in civil society, lessening the security of their enjoyment of the rights which others enjoy, and discriminations which are steps towards reducing them to the condition of a subject race.

That the West Virginia statute respecting juries—the statute that controlled the selection of the grand and petit jury in the case of the plaintiff in error—is such a discrimination ought not to be doubted. Nor would it be if the persons excluded by it were white men. If in those States where the colored people constitute a majority of the entire population a law should be enacted excluding all white men from jury service, thus denying to them the privilege of participating equally with the blacks in the administration of justice, we apprehend no one would be heard to claim that it would not be a denial to white men of the equal protection of the laws. Nor if a law should be passed excluding all naturalized Celtic Irishmen, would there be any doubt of its inconsistency with the spirit of the amendment. The very fact that colored people are singled out and expressly denied by a statute all right to participate in the administration of the law, as jurors, because of their color, though they are citizens, and may be in other respects fully qualified, is practically a brand upon them, affixed by the law, an assertion of their inferiority, and a stimulant to that race prejudice which is an impediment to securing to individuals of the race that equal justice which the law aims to secure to all others.

In view of these considerations, it is hard to see why the statute of West Virginia should not be regarded as discriminating against a colored man when he is put upon trial for an alleged criminal offence against the State. It is not easy to comprehend how it can be said that while every white man is entitled to a trial by a jury selected from persons of his own race or color, or, rather, selected without discrimination against his color, and a negro is not, the latter is equally protected by the law with the former. Is not protection of life and liberty against race or color prejudice, a right, a legal right, under the constitutional amendment? And how can it be maintained that compelling a colored man to submit to a trial for his life by a jury drawn from a panel from which the State has expressly excluded every man of his race, because of color alone, however well qualified in other respects, is not a denial to him of equal legal protection?

BROWN v. BOARD OF EDUCATION, 347 U.S. 483 (1954)

Abridgment of Mr. Chief Justice Warren's Opinion for the Court.

The most avid proponents of the post-War Amendments undoubtedly intended them [in 1868] to remove all legal distinctions among "all persons born or naturalized in the United States." Their opponents, just as certainly, were antagonistic to both the letter and the spirit of the Amendments and wished them to have the most limited effect. What others in Congress and the state legislatures had in mind cannot be determined with any degree of certainty.

An additional reason for the inconclusive nature of the Amendments' history, with respect to segregated schools, is the status of public education at that time. In the South, the movement toward free common schools, supported by general taxation, had not yet taken hold. Education of white children was largely in the hands of private groups. Education of Negroes was almost nonexistent, and practically all of the race were illiterate. In fact, any education of Negroes was forbidden by law in some states. Today, in contrast, many Negroes have achieved outstanding success in the arts and sciences as well as in the business and professional world. It is true that public school education at the time of the Amendment had advanced further in the North, but the effect of the Amendments on Northern States was generally ignored in the congressional debates. Even in the North, the conditions of public education did not approximate those existing today. The curriculum was usually rudimentary; ungraded schools were common in rural areas; the school term was but three months a year in many states; and compulsory school attendance was virtually unknown. As a consequence, it is not surprising that there should be so little in the history of the Fourteenth Amendment relating to its intended effect on public education.

In the first cases in this Court construing the Fourteenth Amendment, decided shortly after its adoption, the Court interpreted it as proscribing all state-imposed discriminations against the Negro race. The doctrine of "separate but equal" did not make its appearance in this Court until 1896 in the case of *Plessy v. Ferguson* involving not education but transportation. . . . In more recent cases, all on the graduate school level, inequality was found in that specific benefits enjoyed by white students were denied to Negro students of the same educational qualifications.

Here . . . there are findings below that the Negro and white schools involved have been equalized, or are being equalized, with respect to buildings, curricula, qualifications and salaries of teachers, and other "tangible" factors. Our decision, therefore, cannot turn on merely a comparison of these tangible factors in the Negro and white schools involved in each of the cases. We must look instead to the effect of segregation itself on public education.

In approaching this problem, we cannot turn the clock back to 1868 when the Amendment was adopted, or even to 1896 when *Plessy v. Ferguson* was written. We must consider public education in the light of its full development and its present place in American life throughout the Nation. Only in this way can it be determined if segregation in public schools deprives these plaintiffs of the equal protection of the laws.

Today, education is perhaps the most important function of state and local governments. [W]here the state has undertaken to provide it, [it] is a right which must be made available to all on equal terms.

In *McLaurin v. Oklahoma State Regents,* the Court, in requiring that a Negro admitted to a white graduate school be treated like all other students, . . . resorted to intangible considerations: ". . . his ability to study, to engage in discussions and exchange views with other students, and, in general, to learn his profession." Such considerations apply with added force to children in grade and high schools. To separate them from others of similar age and qualifications solely because of their race generates a feeling of inferiority as to their status in the community that may affect their hearts and minds in a way unlikely ever to be undone. Whatever may have been the extent of psychological knowledge at the time of *Plessy v. Ferguson,* this finding is amply supported by modern authority. Any language in *Plessy v. Ferguson* contrary to this finding is rejected.

We conclude that in the field of public education the doctrine of "separate but equal" has no place. Separate educational facilities are inherently unequal. Therefore, we hold that the plaintiffs and others similarly situated for whom the actions have been brought are, by reason of the segregation complained of, deprived of the equal protection of the laws guaranteed by the Fourteenth Amendment.

VI

THE RIGHT TO A PUBLIC TRIAL, TO A JURY, TO CONFRONTATION OF WITNESSES, AND TO COUNSEL

In criminal prosecutions, the Sixth Amendment assures the right of the accused to a speedy and public trial by an impartial jury, to be informed of the accusation, to be confronted by the government's witnesses and to call his own witnesses, and to have the assistance of counsel. The Seventh Amendment secures the right to trial by jury in all common law cases where the value in controversy exceeds twenty dollars.

Each of these provisions is binding on trials in the State courts as well as the Federal courts, but the States are free to determine what cases are to be tried without juries in their courts. If a State trial is with a jury, however, it must be an impartial one to meet the test of due process under the Fourteenth Amendment.

Perhaps the most important of these rights, though it is usually taken for granted, is that a trial must be public. The horrors of the Spanish Inquisition of the thirteenth century and the English Court of Star Chamber in the sixteenth and seventeenth centuries exemplify the dangers of secret tribunals.

In 1948 there came to the Supreme Court an appeal from Michigan involving a secret trial. The opinion of the Court reversing the decision expressed surprise and shock that the laws of Michigan could countenance such practice, pointing out that this was the first reported case of a secret trial in the history of the United States and that the last case in England was under Charles I in the early seventeenth century.

The *Oliver* case arose because Michigan had a unique one-man grand jury system. A judge of any court in the State, from the lowest to the highest, could constitute himself a one-man grand jury to investigate alleged crime and return indictments under which the accused then would go to trial with the usual constitutional safeguards. But this one-man grand jury, sitting whenever and wherever he wished, could summon witnesses who appeared before the judge-grand-jury with no one present except the judge's own staff.

In the *Oliver* case, the appellant, when subpoenaed as a witness, did not testify to the satisfaction of the one-man grand jury. Thereupon in accordance with Michigan law, this official said he was no longer sitting as a grand jury but as a judge and, still in secret, sentenced Oliver to sixty days in jail for contempt of court after determining that he had been evasive and untruthful in his answers. And at the end of the sixty days the judge-grand-jury could have subpoenaed the accused again for a secret hearing and have sentenced him to another sixty days if his answers, in this official's sole opinion, were still evasive and untruthful. Indeed, this sixty-day cycle could continue as long as the judge wished.

The Supreme Court did not pass on the right of Michigan to grant traditional inquisitorial grand jury power to a single judge, nor was there a challenge against holding a grand jury investigation in secrecy. The secrecy of grand jury proceedings is a protection of the innocent. But grand juries do not try, convict, and sentence. The Court reversed the *Oliver* conviction, holding that due process was violated in that the defendant did not have a public trial for contempt of court, that he did not have his day in court, namely, reasonable notice of the charge against him and the right to offer testimony, examine witnesses against him, and be represented by counsel. [*In Re Oliver*, 333 U.S. 257 (1948)]

However, this right to a public hearing and to counsel does not extend to a witness before a legislative committee or an administrative agency conducting a fact-finding inquiry. Such a hearing may be secret, and counsel for the witness may be excluded even though the government attorney is present. This secrecy and exclusion of accused's counsel may be enforced even though the purpose of the inquiry is to secure information on which to base a criminal prosecution of the witness.

The New York courts, in an investigation of "ambulance chasing," appointed a New York Supreme Court Justice to take testimony from lawyers, private detectives, and others suspected of criminal practices in reference to accident claims. Two private investigators who were subpoenaed as witnesses before the judge refused to testify because their attorney was excluded from the hearing, though they had been told that whenever they wished they could leave the room to consult their counsel. The United States Supreme Court sustained their contempt convictions, holding that they were not entitled to counsel at the hearing. Justice Black, however, in a dissent in which he was joined by Chief Justice Warren and Justices Douglas and Brennan, said:

> In upholding such secret inquisitions the Court once again retreats from what I conceive to be its highest duty, that of maintaining unimpaired the rights and liberties guaranteed by the Fourteenth Amendment and the Bill of Rights. [*Anonymous v. Baker*, 360 U.S. 287 (1959)]

Although the States are not bound by the jury requirement of the Sixth Amendment, if they do provide trial by jury then the jury must be a fair and impartial one. Otherwise, there is a denial of due process. The Court held that the States may use their own variations of jury trials.

> Some states have taken measures to restrict [the use of juries] . . . ; others . . . diminish the required number of jurors. Some states no longer require the unanimous verdict; others add alternate or substitute jurors to avoid mistrial in case of sickness or death. Some states have abolished the general verdict and require answers to specific questions. [*Fay v. New York*, 332 U.S. 261 (1947)]

Formerly it was the practice in the southern States to exclude Negroes from both trial and grand juries. But after the Supreme Court in case after case reversed convictions where there had been no Negroes on the jury panel, the practice changed substantially. The Court did not hold that when a Negro is indicted or tried there must be Negroes on the jury. The rule is that the jury must be drawn from the population generally, allowing for minimum educational requirements, and then selected without regard to cultural or economic class, race, or religion.

In a recent appeal to the Supreme Court, the record showed that over a period of years in Dallas, Texas, the jury commissioners had consistently limited Negroes selected for grand jury service to not more than one on each grand jury. It was demonstrated that this number was in proportion to the population, but the Court again said that proportional representation of the races was not the proper way to convene a jury. [*Cassell v. Texas;* the Court's opinion, in abridgment, is at page 45.] It is a denial of due process to exclude Negroes as Negroes from jury panels and similarly it is improper to include them as Negroes; jurors are to be selected on an individual basis without regard to race or color.

CASSELL v. TEXAS, 339 U.S. 282 (1950)

Abridgment of Mr. Justice Reed's Opinion for the Court. (Mr. Justice Frankfurter with whom Mr. Justice Burton and Mr. Justice Minton joined and Mr. Justice Clark concurred in separate opinions. Mr. Justice Jackson dissented. Mr. Justice Douglas took no part in the case.)

Review was sought in this case to determine whether there has been a violation by Texas of petitioner's federal constitutional right to a fair and impartial grand jury.

Since the *Hill* case [316 U. S. 400 (1942)] the judges of the trial court have been careful to instruct their jury commissioners that discrimination on grounds of race or color is forbidden. The judge did so here. If, notwithstanding this caution by the trial court judges, commissioners should limit proportionally the number of Negroes selected for grand-jury service, such limitation would violate our Constitution. Jurymen should be selected as individuals, on the basis of individual qualifications, and not as members of a race.

We have recently written why proportional representation of races on a jury is not a constitutional requisite. Succinctly stated, our reason was that the Constitution requires only a fair jury selected without regard to race. Obviously the number of races and nationalities appearing in the ancestry of our citizens would make it impossible to meet a requirement of proportional representation. Similarly, since there can be no exclusion of Negroes as a race and no discrimination because of color, proportional limitation is not permissible. That conclusion is compelled by the United States Code, Title 18, §243, based on §4 of the Civil Rights Act of 1875. While the language of the section directs attention to the right to serve as a juror, its command has long been recognized also to assure rights to an accused. Prohibiting racial disqualification of Negroes for jury service, this congressional enactment under the Fourteenth Amendment, §5, has been consistently sustained and its violation held to deny a proper trial to a Negro accused. Proportional racial limitation is therefore forbidden. An accused is entitled to have charges against him considered by a jury in the selection of which there has been neither inclusion nor exclusion because of race.

[The record shows that since the *Hill* case in 1942 and 1947, when petitioner was indicted, there had been 21 grand juries on none of which there was more than one Negro, and that this was in

proportion to the eligible Negro and white voters in the county.]
Our holding that there was discrimination in the selection of grand
jurors in this case, however, is based on another ground. In ex-
plaining the fact that no Negroes appeared on this grand-jury list, the
commissioners said that they knew none available who qualified; at
the same time they said they chose jurymen only from those
people with whom they were personally acquainted. It may be assumed that in ordinary activities in Dallas County, acquaintanceship
between the races is not on a sufficiently familiar basis to give citizens eligible for appointment as jury commissioners an opportunity to
know the qualifications for grand-jury service of many members of
another race. An individual's qualifications for grand-jury service,
however, are not hard to ascertain, and with no evidence to the
contrary, we must assume that a large proportion of the Negroes of
Dallas County met the statutory requirements for jury service. When
the commissioners were appointed as judicial administrative officials,
it was their duty to familiarize themselves fairly with the qualifications of the eligible jurors of the county without regard to race and
color.

The existence of the kind of discrimination described in the *Hill*
case does not depend upon systematic exclusion continuing over a
long period and practiced by a succession of jury commissioners.
Since the issue must be whether there has been discrimination in the
selection of the jury that has indicted petitioner, it is enough to have
direct evidence based on the statements of the jury commissioners
in the very case. Discrimination may be proved in other ways than
by evidence of long-continued unexplained absence of Negroes from
many panels. The statements of the jury commissioners that they
chose only whom they knew, and that they knew no eligible Negroes
in an area where Negroes made up so large a proportion of the
population, prove the intentional exclusion that is discrimination in
violation of petitioner's constitutional rights.

The judgment of the Court of Criminal Appeals of Texas is
reversed.

VII

PROTECTION AGAINST
SELF INCRIMINATION

The privilege against self incrimination, which is found in the Fifth Amendment provision that a person may not be "compelled in any Criminal Case to be a witness against himself," has its origins in the reaction against the heresy prosecutions of the thirteenth-century Inquisition and in the persecution of the Puritans in England before they emigrated to the New World. The heresy prosecutions were conducted in secret. The defendant was not told the identity of his accusers, and the testimony of professional spies, children, and the demented was given full credence. The defendant was commanded to testify, and not uncommonly tortured if his answers were not responsive to the accusations made against him, even though these had not been communicated to him.

In 1641, in *Lilburne's Case* [16 Car. I, Ch. 10], the British Parliament, reversing a religious nonconformist's conviction for refusal to testify when he was accused before the Court of Star Chamber, established the rule in Anglo-Saxon law that one may not be required to testify against himself.

The prohibition of the Fifth Amendment, which speaks of compulsory testimony in a criminal case, has been held by the Supreme Court to mean that testimony may not be required in any case, civil or criminal, or even before an administrative agency or Congressional committee, if such testimony may either directly incriminate the witness or be a link in a chain which might result in the witness being prosecuted for a crime. [*Emspak v. United States;* the Court's opinion, in abridgment, is at page 51.] This immunity against compulsory testimony includes the witness's records and papers other than those he may be required to maintain by law. The privilege would not, for example, extend to a pharmacist's record of certain drug inventories and sales.

In the Federal courts and most of the State courts, neither the judge nor the prosecutor may comment to the jury on the defendant's failure to testify. No presumption of guilt is to be drawn from the defendant's invoking the protection of the Fifth Amendment. But Fifth Amendment rights are Federal only; the prohibition against compulsory testimony is not a restriction against the States. This is the present rule, although there is opinion to the contrary in which at least two Justices of the Supreme Court join. However, forty-eight of the fifty States have in their own constitutions similar prohibitions against compulsory testimony, and the other two States (New Jersey and Iowa) recognize the doctrine as part of their common law, referring back to *Lilburne's Case,* which Parliament decided while some of the original thirteen States were English colonies.

Because there are situations where a witness's testimony may be more important to the government than his prosecution for an offense he may have committed, there are statutes under which he may be compelled to testify if he is granted immunity from prosecution. Such statutes have been held constitutional when they give total immunity but not when the protection is partial. Insufficient immunity was granted by a law which prohibited the use of the witness's testimony in subsequent prosecution but still permitted a prosecution for the acts concerning which he testified.

Despite the prohibitions against compelling testimony in both the Federal Constitution and in the constitutions or laws of each of the States, there is an area in which neither protection applies. The privilege may be invoked in a Federal court only when the self incrimination would be in reference to a Federal offense, and similarly a witness may refuse to answer in most State courts only to protect himself against State prosecution. He may not refuse to answer in a Federal court or before a Federal agency or committee on the ground that his testimony may incriminate him in reference to a State law. The converse is also true: a witness in most State courts may not invoke the privilege against self-incrimination in reference to a Federal crime.

This anomaly arises from the history of the Bill of Rights. When adopted, the first eight Amendments were intended as restrictions against the Federal government and not as limitations on State action. The colonists did not fear their own States; they were concerned only that the new Federal government they were creating might deprive them of their liberties. The 1789 Congress, which proposed the Amendments for ratification, refused in the Senate to include one which provided: "No State shall infringe the equal rights of conscience, nor the freedom of speech or of the press, nor the right of trial by jury in criminal cases."

The Thirteenth, Fourteenth, and Fifteenth Amendments, however, are by their language binding on the States. These include the prohibitions against slavery and discrimination in voting, and the guaranties of equal protection of the laws and due process of law.

The Supreme Court, in a line of decisions beginning in the 1920's, utilized the Fourteenth Amendment, which prohibits State action in violation of due process of law, to establish the doctrine that the States are constitutionally prohibited from interfering with the basic individual liberties such as freedom of speech, the press, and religion. [*Gilbert v. Minnesota,* 254 U.S. 325 (1920); *Palko v. Connecticut,* 302 U.S. 319 (1937)]

It is on theory possible to argue that this prohibition was a usurpation by the Federal government of power which was refused it when the Constitution was adopted. The Court, however, recognizing the Constitution as a vibrant, dynamic instrument for the protection of an ever-changing society, and realizing that in the needs of life today a stronger federalism is required than may have been envisaged in 1789, has protected "the fundamental personal liberties" from the dangers of State action or sectionalism.

However, the Court has not included within the purview of the Fourteenth Amendment the entire first eight Amendments, thereby making all these liberties binding on the States. Two of the present Supreme Court Justices, Black and Douglas, time and again in both dissenting and concurring opinions have stated their position that the entire Bill of Rights has been binding on the States since the adoption of the Fourteenth Amendment. [*Adamson v. California;* Justice Black's dissenting opinion, in abridgment, is at page 55.] Perhaps in time this view will become that of the Court majority.

Convictions have been obtained on confessions procured from the accused by police brutality, by questioning for hours and even days while under glaring electric lights, through fraud and trickery, and while being held incommunicado for an unreasonable length of time before being arraigned. Such confessions have been held to be inadmissible as evidence. The Supreme Court in a number of cases has reversed convictions, holding that such police action is a violation of the personal immunities which are "implicit in the concept of ordered liberty" and violative of the due process clause of the Fourteenth Amendment. In a recent case, in which incriminating evidence, swallowed by the accused at the time of his arrest, was recovered with a stomach pump, the Court reversed the conviction, holding that the use of this evidence was a denial of due process. [*Rochin v. California;* the Court's opinion, in abridgment, is at page 60.] Justices Black and Douglas based their concurring opinion on the Fifth Amendment prohibition against self incrimination, saying again that the Bill of Rights was binding on the States in its entirety.

EMSPAK v. UNITED STATES,
349 U.S. 190 (1955)

*Abridgment of Mr. Chief Justice Warren's Opinion for the Court.
(Mr. Justice Reed dissented in an opinion in which Mr. Justice
Minton concurred. Mr. Justice Harlan dissented in a separate
opinion.)*

Pursuant to subpoena, petitioner appeared on December 5, 1949,
before a subcommittee of the Committee on Un-American Activities.
The subcommittee consisted of a single member, Rep. Morgan M.
Moulder. Petitioner was then the General Secretary-Treasurer of the
United Electrical, Radio & Machine Workers of America as well as
Editor of the *UE News,* the union's official publication. The subcommittee's hearings had previously been announced as concerning
"the question of Communist affiliation or association of certain members" of the union and "the advisability of tightening present security
requirements in industrial plants working on certain Government
contracts."

Petitioner was asked a total of 239 questions. Most dealt with the
structure of the union, the duties of its officers, the scope of its
membership and bargaining commitments, the alleged similarity in
policies of the *UE News* and the Communist Party, the non-
Communist affidavit that petitioner had filed with the National Labor
Relations Board, and related matters. Petitioner answered all of these
questions. He declined, however, to answer 68 of the 239 questions.
These 68 questions dealt exclusively with petitioner's associations and
affiliations. He based his refusal on "primarily the first amendment,
supplemented by the fifth." Of the 68 questions, 58 asked in substance that he state whether or not he was acquainted with certain
named individuals and whether or not those individuals had ever
held official positions in the union. Two of the questions concerned
petitioner's alleged membership in the National Federation for Constitutional Liberties and the Civil Rights Congress. Eight questions
concerned petitioner's alleged membership and activity in the Communist Party.

On November 20, 1950, petitioner was indicted . . . for his refusal
to answer the 68 questions . . . .

As pointed out in *Quinn v. United States,* no ritualistic formula
or talismanic phrase is essential in order to invoke the privilege
against self-incrimination. All that is necessary is an objection stated

in language that a committee may reasonably be expected to understand as an attempt to invoke the privilege. In the *Quinn* case we hold that Quinn's references to "the First and Fifth Amendments" and "the First Amendment to the Constitution, supplemented by the Fifth Amendment" were sufficient to meet this standard. It would be unwarranted, we think, to reach a different conclusion here as to petitioner's plea based on "primarily the first amendment, supplemented by the fifth."

The Government does not even attempt to distinguish between the two cases in this respect. Apparently conceding that petitioner as well as Quinn *intended* to invoke the privilege, the Government points out "the probability" that his references to the Fifth Amendment were likewise deliberately phrased in muffled terms "to obtain the benefit of the privilege without incurring the popular opprobrium which often attaches to its exercise." On this basis the Government contends that petitioner's plea was not adequate. The answer to this contention is threefold. First, an objection that is sufficiently clear to reveal a probable intention to invoke the privilege cannot be ignored merely because it is not phrased in an orthodox manner. Second, if it is true that in these times a stigma may somehow result from a witness' reliance on the Self-Incrimination Clause, a committee should be all the more ready to recognize a veiled claim of the privilege. Otherwise, the great right which the Clause was intended to secure might be effectively frustrated by private pressures. Third, it should be noted that a committee is not obliged to either accept or reject an ambiguous constitutional claim the very moment it is first presented. The way is always open for the committee to inquire into the nature of the claim before making a ruling. If the witness intelligently and unequivocally waives any objection based on the Self-Incrimination Clause, or if the witness refuses a committee request to state whether he relies on the Self-Incrimination Clause, he cannot later invoke its protection in a prosecution for contempt for refusing to answer that question.

The Government argues that petitioner did in fact waive the privilege, at least as to one count of the indictment, and that the conviction can be sustained on that count alone. In response to a question concerning his associations, petitioner expressed apprehension that the committee was "trying to perhaps frame people for possible criminal prosecution" and added that "I think I have the right to reserve whatever rights I have. . . ." The following colloquy then took place:

"Mr. Moulder. Is it your feeling that to reveal your knowledge of them would subject you to criminal prosecution?

"Mr. Emspak. No. I don't think this committee has a right to pry into my associations. That is my own position."

Petitioner's reply, it is contended, constituted an effective disclaimer of the privilege. We find this contention without merit.

... [I]n the instant case, we do not think that petitioner's "No" answer can be treated as a waiver of his previous express claim under the Fifth Amendment. At most ... petitioner's "No" is equivocal. It may have merely represented a justifiable refusal to discuss the reasons underlying petitioner's assertion of the privilege; the privilege would be of little avail if a witness invoking it were required to disclose the precise hazard which he fears. And even if petitioner's "No" answer were taken as responsive to the question, the answer would still be consistent with a claim of the privilege. The protection of the Self-Incrimination Clause is not limited to admissions that "would subject [a witness] to criminal prosecution"; for this Court has repeatedly held that "Whether such admissions by themselves would support a conviction under a criminal statute is immaterial" and that the privilege also extends to admissions that may only tend to incriminate. ...

"To sustain the privilege," this Court has recently held, "it need only be evident from the implications of the question, in the setting in which it is asked, that a responsive answer to the question or an explanation of why it cannot be answered might be dangerous because injurious disclosure could result." And nearly 150 years ago Chief Justice Marshall enunciated a similar test: "Many links frequently compose that chain of testimony which is necessary to convict any individual of a crime. It appears to the court to be the true sense of the rule that no witness is compellable to furnish any one of them against himself." Applying this test to the instant case, we have no doubt that the eight questions concerning petitioner's alleged membership in the Communist Party fell within the scope of the privilege. The same is true of the two questions concerning petitioner's alleged membership in the National Federation for Constitutional Liberties and the Civil Rights Congress; both organizations had previously been cited by the committee as Communist-front organizations. There remains for consideration the 58 questions concerning petitioner's associations. This Court has already made abundantly clear that such questions, when asked in a setting of possible incrimination, may fall within the scope of the privilege. What was the setting—as revealed by the record—in which these questions were asked? Each of the named individuals had previously been charged with having Communist affiliations. On October 14, 1949, less than two months prior to petitioner's appearance before the committee, eleven principal leaders of the Communist Party in this country had been convicted under the Smith Act for conspiring to teach and advocate the violent overthrow of the United States. Petitioner was identified at their trial as a Communist and an associate of the defendants. It was reported that Smith Act indictments against other Communist leaders were being prepared. On November 23, 1949, two weeks prior to petitioner's appearance, newspapers carried the story that the Department of Justice "within thirty days" would take "an important step" toward the criminal prosecution of petitioner in connection with his non-Communist affidavit filed with the National Labor Relations Board.

Under these circumstances, it seems clear that answers to the 58 questions concerning petitioner's associations "might be dangerous because injurious disclosure could result." To reveal knowledge about the named individuals—all of them having been previously charged with Communist affiliations—could well have furnished "a link in the chain" of evidence needed to prosecute petitioner for a federal crime, ranging from conspiracy to violate the Smith Act to the filing of a false non-Communist affidavit under the Taft-Hartley Act. That being so, it is immaterial that some of the questions sought information about associations that petitioner might have been able to explain away on some innocent basis unrelated to Communism. If an answer to a question may tend to be incriminatory, a witness is not deprived of the protection of the privilege merely because the witness if subsequently prosecuted could perhaps refute any inference of guilt arising from the answer.

ADAMSON v. CALIFORNIA,
332 U.S. 46 (1947)

Abridgment of Mr. Justice Black's Dissenting Opinion with whom Mr. Justice Douglas concurred. (Mr. Justice Murphy dissented in a separate opinion.)

The appellant was tried for murder in a California state court. He did not take the stand as a witness in his own behalf. The prosecuting attorney, under purported authority of a California statute, argued to the jury that an inference of guilt could be drawn because of appellant's failure to deny evidence offered against him. The appellant's contention in the state court and here has been that the statute denies him a right guaranteed by the Federal Constitution. The argument is that (1) permitting comment upon his failure to testify has the effect of compelling him to testify so as to violate that provision of the Bill of Rights contained in the Fifth Amendment that "No person . . . shall be compelled in any criminal case to be a witness against himself"; and (2) although this provision of the Fifth Amendment originally applied only as a restraint upon federal courts, the Fourteenth Amendment was intended to, and did, make the prohibition against compelled testimony applicable to trials in state courts.

The Court refuses to meet and decide the appellant's first contention. But while the Court's opinion, as I read it, strongly implies that the Fifth Amendment does not, of itself, bar comment upon failure to testify in federal courts, the Court nevertheless assumes that it does in order to reach the second constitutional question involved in appellant's case. I must consider the case on the same assumption that the Court does. For the discussion of the second contention turns out to be a decision which reaches far beyond the relatively narrow issues on which this case might have turned.

This decision reasserts a constitutional theory spelled out in *Twining v. New Jersey*, 211 U.S. 78, that this Court is endowed by the Constitution with boundless power under "natural law" periodically to expand and contract constitutional standards to conform to the Court's conception of what at a particular time constitutes "civilized decency" and "fundamental liberty and justice." Invoking this *Twining* rule, the Court concludes that although comment upon testimony in a federal court would violate the Fifth Amendment, identical comment in a state court does not violate today's fashion in civilized decency and fundamentals and is therefore not prohibited by the Federal Constitution as amended.

The *Twining* case was the first, as it is the only, decision of this Court which has squarely held that states were free, notwithstanding the Fifth and Fourteenth Amendments, to exort evidence from one accused of crime. I agree that if *Twining* be reaffirmed, the result reached might appropriately follow. But I would not reaffirm the *Twining* decision. I think that decision and the "natural law" theory of the constitution upon which it relies degrade the constitutional safeguards of the Bill of Rights and simultaneously appropriate for this Court a broad power which we are not authorized by the Constitution to exercise. . . . My reasons for believing that the *Twining* decision should not be revitalized can best be understood by reference to the constitutional, judicial, and general history that preceded and followed the case. That reference must be abbreviated far more than is justified but for the necessary limitations of opinion-writing.

The first ten amendments were proposed and adopted largely because of fear that Government might unduly interfere with prized individual liberties. The people wanted and demanded a Bill of Rights written into their Constitution. The amendments embodying the Bill of Rights were intended to curb all branches of the Federal Government in the fields touched by the amendments—Legislative, Executive, and Judicial. The Fifth, Sixth and Eighth Amendments were pointedly aimed at confining exercise of power by courts and judges within precise boundaries, particularly in the procedure used for the trial of criminal cases. Past history provided strong reasons for the apprehensions which brought these procedural amendments into being and attest the wisdom of their adoption. For the fears of arbitrary court action sprang largely from the past use of courts in the imposition of criminal punishments to suppress speech, press, and religion. Hence the constitutional limitations of courts' powers were, in the view of the Founders, essential supplements to the First Amendment, which was itself designed to protect the widest scope for all people to believe and to express the most divergent political, religious, and other views.

But these limitations were not expressly imposed upon state court action. In 1833, . . . the Court . . . said that it could not hold that the first eight amendments applied to the states. This was the controlling constitutional rule when the Fourteenth Amendment was proposed in 1866.

My study of the historical events that culminated in the Four-

teenth Amendment, and the expressions of those who sponsored and
favored, as well as those who opposed its submission and passage,
persuades me that one of the chief objects that the provisions of the
Amendment's first section, separately, and as a whole, were intended
to accomplish was to make the Bill of Rights, applicable to the states.
With full knowledge of the import of the [1833] decision, the
framers and backers of the Fourteenth Amendment proclaimed its
purpose to be to overturn the constitutional rule that case had announced. This historical purpose has never received full consideration or exposition in any opinion of this Court interpreting the
Amendment.

In construing other constitutional provisions, this Court has almost
uniformly followed the precept . . . "It is never to be forgotten that,
in the construction of the language of the Constitution . . . , as indeed in all other instances where construction becomes necessary, we
are to place ourselves as nearly as possible in the condition of the
men who framed that instrument."

In the *Twining* opinion, the Court explicitly declined to give
weight to the historical demonstration that the first section of the
Amendment was intended to apply to the states the several protections of the Bill of Rights. It held that that question was "no longer
open" because of previous decisions of this Court which, however,
had not appraised the historical evidence on that subject. The Court
admitted that its action had resulted in giving "much less effect to
the Fourteenth Amendment than some of the public men active
in framing it" had intended it to have. With particular reference to
the guarantee against compelled testimony, the Court stated that
"Much might be said in favor of the view that the privilege was
guaranteed against state impairment as a privilege and immunity of
National citizenship, but, as has been shown, the decisions of this
court have foreclosed that view." Thus the Court declined, and again
today declines, to appraise the relevant historical evidence of the intended scope of the first section of the Amendment. Instead it relied
upon previous cases, none of which had analyzed the evidence showing that one purpose of those who framed, advocated, and adopted
the Amendment had been to make the Bill of Rights applicable to
the States. None of the cases relied upon by the Court today made
such an analysis.

For this reason, I am attaching to this dissent an appendix which
contains a resume, by no means complete, of the Amendment's history. In my judgment that history conclusively demonstrates that the

language of the first section of the Fourteenth Amendment, taken as a whole, was thought by those responsible for its submission to the people, and by those who opposed its submission, sufficiently explicit, to guarantee that thereafter no state could deprive its citizens of the privileges and protections of the Bill of Rights. Whether this Court ever will, or whether it now should, in the light of past decisions, give full effect to what the Amendment was intended to accomplish is not necessarily essential to a decision here. However that may be, our prior decisions, including *Twining*, do not prevent our carrying out that purpose, at least to the extent of making applicable to the states, not a mere part, as the Court has, but the full protection of the Fifth Amendment's provision against compelling evidence from an accused to convict him of crime. And I further contend that the "natural law" formula which the Court uses to reach its conclusion in this case should be abandoned as an incongruous excrescence on our Constitution. I believe that formula to be itself a violation of our Constitution, in that it subtly conveys to courts, at the expense of legislatures, ultimate power over public policies in fields where no specific provision of the Constitution limits legislative power. And my belief seems to be in accord with the views expressed by this Court, at least for the first two decades after the Fourteenth Amendment was adopted.

I cannot consider the Bill of Rights to be an outworn 18th Century "strait jacket" as the *Twining* opinion did. Its provisions may be thought outdated abstractions by some. And it is true that they were designed to meet ancient evils. But they are the same kind of human evils that have emerged from century to century wherever excessive power is sought by the few at the expense of the many. In my judgment the people of no nation can lose their liberty so long as a Bill of Rights like ours survives and its basic purposes are conscientiously interpreted, enforced and respected so as to afford continuous protection against old, as well as new, devices and practices which might thwart those purposes. I fear to see the consequences of the Court's practice of substituting its own concepts of decency and fundamental justice for the language of the Bill of Rights as its point of departure in interpreting and enforcing that Bill of Rights. If the choice must be between the selective process of the *Palko* decision applying some of the Bill of Rights to the States, or the *Twining* rule applying none of them, I would choose the *Palko* selective process. But rather than accept either of these choices, I would follow what I believe was the original purpose of the Fourteenth Amendment—to extend to all the people of the nation the complete protection of the Bill of Rights. To hold that this Court can determine what, if any, provisions of the Bill of Rights will be enforced, and if so to what degree, is to frustrate the great design of a written Constitution.

ROCHIN v. CALIFORNIA, 342 U.S. 165 (1952)

Abridgment of Mr. Justice Frankfurter's Opinion for the Court. (Mr. Justice Black and Mr. Justice Douglas concurred in separate opinions.)

Having "some information that [the petitioner here] was selling narcotics," three deputy sheriffs of the County of Los Angeles, on the morning of July 1, 1949, made for the two-story dwelling house in which Rochin lived. . . . Finding the outside door open, they entered and then forced open the door to Rochin's room on the second floor. Inside they found petitioner sitting partly dressed on the side of the bed. . . . On a "night stand" beside the bed the deputies spied two capsules. Rochin seized the capsules and put them in his mouth. He was handcuffed and taken to a hospital. At the direction of one of the officers a doctor forced an emetic solution through a tube into Rochin's stomach against his will. This "stomach pumping" produced vomiting. In the vomited matter were found two capsules which proved to contain morphine.

[W]e are compelled to conclude that the proceedings by which this conviction was obtained do more than offend some fastidious squeamishness or private sentimentalism about combatting crime too energetically. This is conduct that shocks the conscience. Illegally breaking into the privacy of the petitioner, the struggle to open his mouth and remove what was there, the forcible extraction of his stomach's contents—this course of proceeding by agents of government to obtain evidence is bound to offend even hardened sensibilities. They are methods too close to the rack and the screw to permit of constitutional differentiation.

It has long since ceased to be true that due process of law is heedless of the means by which otherwise relevant and credible evidence is obtained. This was not true even before the series of recent cases enforced the constitutional principle that the States may not base convictions upon confessions, however much verified, obtained by coercion. These decisions are not arbitrary exceptions to the comprehensive right of States to fashion their own rules of evidence for criminal trials. They are not sports in our constitutional law but applications of a general principle. They are only instances of the general requirement that States in their prosecutions respect certain decencies of civilized conduct. It would be a stultification of the responsibility which the course of constitutional history has cast upon this Court to hold that in order to convict a man the police cannot extract by force what is in his mind but can extract what is in his stomach.

To attempt in this case to distinguish what lawyers call "real evidence" from verbal evidence is to ignore the reasons for excluding coerced confessions. Use of involuntary verbal confessions in State criminal trials is constitutionally obnoxious not only because of their unreliability. They are inadmissible under the Due Process Clause even though statements contained in them may be independently established as true. Coerced confessions offend the community's sense of fair play and decency. So here, to sanction the brutal conduct which naturally enough was condemned by the court whose judgment is before us, would be to afford brutality the cloak of law.

The judgment below must be Reversed.

VIII

PROTECTION AGAINST UNLAWFUL SEARCH AND SEIZURE—WIRE TAPPING

The origin of the Fourth Amendment can be traced to the activities of the Star Chamber, which was first established as a council to hear judicial matters addressed to the King. Under Charles I, who ruled for years as an absolute monarch, the Chamber developed into an inquisitorial body which tortured the accused for confessions, after searching their homes and seizing their papers. The Star Chamber initiated the "general warrant" directing its officers to seize all papers in the homes of those suspected of disloyalty to the Crown. Prior to this period, substantial respect had been paid to the maxim that every man's home is his castle, and no one could enter it except with a search warrant directed to specific papers or property such as stolen goods or contraband. The House of Commons affirmed a court decision holding the Star Chamber's general warrants invalid, but a century later in the American colonies the use of general warrants was again invoked. Concerning the colonists' protest against these searches without warrants and against searches with warrants unlimited in scope, John Adams said, "American independence was then and there born."

The draftsmen of the Bill of Rights were acquainted with this history, and in the Fourth Amendment secured the people, their houses, papers, and effects against unreasonable search and seizure, providing that warrants shall issue only upon probable cause and shall be particular, not general, in describing place, persons, and things.

Even the right of search, at the time of arrest, of the place where the arrest is made has been limited by the Court to those things which might have been seized if a search warrant had been secured. A 1951 decision is in point: Without a warrant but with reason to believe narcotics were concealed there, a hotel detective and a District of Columbia police officer entered the room of defendant Jeffers' aunt and seized narcotics, the property of defendant. The Court held that while Jeffers had no "property" right in the narcotics, such as would entitle him to their return, the drugs were his "property" within the purview of the Fourth Amendment protection of the security of one's person, house, papers and effects. [*United States v. Jeffers*, 342 U.S. 48 (1951)]

But some searches are not "unreasonable" and may be made without a warrant. Each situation must be decided on its own facts, by weighing the nature of the offense, the danger of the suspect's fleeing, the evidence available prior to the search, and the likelihood of the later availability of the property or papers for which the search was made. [*Frank v. Maryland;* an abridgment of the Court's opinion is at page 66 and of a dissenting opinion at page 67.]

Evidence secured in violation of the Fourth Amendment may not be used in a Federal or State court. The Court has held that a person's privacy and protection against unreasonable search is a fundamental right in a free society and that, therefore, the Fourth Amendment is binding on the States by enforcement of the due process clause of the Fourteenth Amendment. [*Mapp v. Ohio;* an abridgment of the Court's Opinion is at page 69.]

Wire tapping in an early case was held not to be within the contemplation of the Fourth Amendment. [*Olmstead v. United States*, 277 U.S. 438 (1928)] A minority of the Justices said it was as much an unlawful search as invading a person's home, differing only in that it used modern technology. This dissenting view is reflected in the present Federal Communications Act (Section 605) which provides that "no person not being authorized by the sender shall intercept any communication and divulge or publish the existence . . . or meaning . . . to any person." Today it is that statute and not the Bill of Rights that prohibits the use in a Federal court of evidence produced by wire tapping.

The *Olmstead* case created the odd situation that when State police officers, in violation of the Communications Act, tap a person's telephone there is no prohibition of the use of the evidence in a State court unless trial procedures of the State itself prohibit its use. [*Schwartz v. Texas,* 344 U.S. 199 (1953)] Only five of the States will not receive evidence in court that was obtained by wire tapping; Illinois, Pennsylvania, and Rhode Island have statutes prohibiting all wire tapping, including police taps, and the courts of California and Florida, as part of their trial procedural rules, refuse to accept evidence obtained through wire tapping. All the other States allow wire taps to be used as evidence even though they were obtained in violation of the Federal Communications Act. The only other limitation is that five States (Massachusetts, Maryland, Nevada, New York, and Oregon) require police officers to first secure a court order authorizing the wire tapping.

The Court, in 1957, held that the prohibitions of the Federal Communications Act were binding on the States and supersede the New York law. Nevertheless, under the doctrine that the Court should not interfere with the procedural rules of the State courts, the Court confirmed a conviction based on wire-tap evidence. [*United States v. Benanti,* 355 U.S. 96 (1957)] The Court almost gratuitously added that the police officers were subject to prosecution for violating the Federal Communications Act. If that pronouncement was of any comfort to Benanti or a deterrent to any police officers it was soon dissipated by the Attorney General's announcing that he would not order any such prosecutions. The final result is that police officers wire tap with impunity in violation of an act of Congress and a holding of the Court. And in further violation of this Federal criminal statute courts receive wire-tap evidence with the blessing of the Supreme Court's holding that it cannot interfere with the rules of procedure of State courts.

This anomaly is in contradiction of the action of the Court in the 1961 *Mapp* case which reversed its former rule [*Wolf v. Colorado,* 338 U.S. 25 (1949)] and held that evidence secured by an illegal search was barred from use in State courts by the due process requirements of the Fourteenth Amendment. It is suggested that the Court, though it may refuse jurisdiction for some time, ultimately will recognize that wire tapping is nothing more nor less than a search with modern technology. From this recognition it would follow that the admissibility of wire-tap evidence is not to be determined by State court rules of procedure but is within the protection of the due process clause of the Fourteenth Amendment.

FRANK v. MARYLAND,
359 U.S. 360 (1959)

*Abridgment of Mr. Justice Frankfurter's Opinion for the Court.
(Mr. Justice Whittaker concurred in a separate opinion.)*

Acting on a complaint from a resident of . . . Baltimore, Maryland, that there were rats in her basement, Gentry, an inspector of the Baltimore City Health Department, began an inspection of the houses in the vicinity looking for the source of the rats. In the middle of the afternoon of February 27, 1958, Gentry knocked on the door of appellant's . . . home. . . . After receiving no response he proceeded to inspect the area outside the house. During this inspection appellant came around the side of the house and asked Gentry to explain his presence. Gentry responded that he had evidence of rodent infestation and asked appellant for permission to inspect the basement area. Appellant refused. At no time did Gentry have a warrant authorizing him to enter. He . . . swore out a warrant for appellant's arrest alleging a violation of § 120 of Art. 12 of the Baltimore City Code.

The power of inspection granted by the Baltimore City Code is strictly limited, more exacting than the analogous provisions of many other municipal codes. Valid grounds for suspicion of the existence of a nuisance must exist. The inspection must be made in the daytime. A fine is imposed for resistance, but officials are not authorized to break past the unwilling occupant.

Thus, not only does the inspection touch at most upon the periphery of the important interests safeguarded by the Fourteenth Amendment's protection against official intrusion, but it is hedged about with safeguards designed to make the least possible demand on the individual occupant, and to cause only the slightest restriction on his claims of privacy. Such a demand must be assessed in the light of the needs which have produced it.

Time and experience have forcefully taught that the power to inspect dwelling places, either as a matter of systematic area-by-area search or, as here, to treat a specific problem, is of indispensable importance to the maintenance of community health; a power that would be greatly hobbled by the blanket requirement of the safeguards necessary for a search of evidence of criminal acts. The need for preventive action is great, and city after city has seen this need and granted the power of inspection to its health officials, and these

inspections are apparently welcomed by all but an insignificant few.
In the light of the long history of this kind of inspection and of
modern needs, we cannot say that the carefully circumscribed demand which Maryland here makes on appellant's freedom has deprived him of due process of law.
Affirmed.

*Abridgment of Dissenting Opinion of Mr. Justice Douglas (with
whom Mr. Chief Justice Warren, Mr. Justice Black, and Mr. Justice
Brennan concurred)*:

The decision today greatly dilutes the right of privacy which every
homeowner had the right to believe was part of our American heritage. We witness indeed an inquest over a substantial part of the
Fourth Amendment.

The court said in *Wolf v. Colorado* that "The security of one's
privacy against arbitrary intrusion by the police—which is at the core
of the Fourth Amendment—is basic to a free society." Now that re-
sounding phrase is watered down to embrace only certain invasions
of one's privacy. If officials come to inspect sanitary conditions, they
may come without a warrant and demand entry as of right. This is
a strange deletion to make from the Fourth Amendment. In some
States the health inspectors are none other than the police themselves. In some States the presence of unsanitary conditions gives rise
to criminal prosecutions. The knock on the door in any health inspection case may thus lay the groundwork for a criminal prosecution. The resistance of the citizen in the present case led to the imposition of a fine. If a fine may be imposed, why not a prison term?

It is said, however, that this fine is so small as to amount only to
an assessment to cover the costs of the inspection. The truth is that
the amount of the fine is not the measure of the right. The right is
the guarantee against invasion of the home by officers without a warrant. No officer of government is authorized to penalize the citizen
because he invokes his constitutional protection.

We live in an era "when politically controlled officials have grown
powerful through an ever increasing series of minor infractions of
civil liberties." One invasion of privacy by an official of government can be as oppressive as another. Health inspections are important. But they are hardly more important than the search for
narcotic peddlers, rapists, kidnapers, murderers, and other criminal
elements. Many today would think that the search for subversives

was even more important than the search for unsanitary conditions. It would seem that the public interest in protecting privacy is equally as great in one case as in another. The fear that health inspections will suffer if constitutional safeguards are applied is strongly held by some. Like notions obtain by some law enforcement officials who take shortcuts in pursuit of criminals. The same pattern appears over and again whenever government seeks to use its compulsive force against the citizen.

Certainly this is a poor case for dispensing with the need for a search warrant. Evidence to obtain one was abundant. The house was in a state of extreme decay; and in the rear of the house was a pile of "rodent feces mixed with straw and debris to approximately half a ton." This is not to suggest that a health official need show the same kind of proof to a magistrate to obtain a warrant as one must who would search for the fruits or instrumentalities of crime. Where considerations of health and safety are involved, the facts that would justify an inference of "probable cause" to make an inspection are clearly different from those that would justify such an inference where a criminal investigation has been undertaken.

England—a nation no less mindful of public health than we and keenly conscious of civil liberties—has long proceeded on the basis that where the citizen denies entrance to a health inspector, a search warrant is needed.

We cannot do less and still be true to the command of the Fourth Amendment which protects even the lowliest home in the land from intrusion on the mere say-so of an official.

MAPP v. OHIO, 367 U.S. 643 (1961)

Abridgment of Mr. Justice Clark's Opinion for the Court. (Mr. Justice Harlan dissented in an opinion in which Mr. Justice Frankfurter and Mr. Justice Whittaker concurred. Mr. Justice Stewart dissented in a memorandum but voted with the majority to reverse the conviction.)

The State says that even if the search were made without authority, or otherwise unreasonably, it is not prevented from using the unconstitutionally seized evidence at trial, citing *Wolf v. Colorado,* in which this court did indeed hold "that in a prosecution in a State court for a State crime the Fourteenth Amendment does not forbid the admission of evidence obtained by a unreasonable search and seizure." On this appeal, of which we have noted probable jurisdiction, it is urged once again that we review that holding.

Thus, in the year 1914, in the *Weeks* case this court "for the first time" held that "in a federal prosecution the Fourth Amendment barred the use of evidence secured through an illegal search and seizure."

This court has ever since required of federal law officers a strict adherence to that command which this Court has held to be a clear, specific, and constitutionally required—even if judicially implied— deterrent safeguard without insistence upon which the Fourth Amendment would have been reduced to "a form of words." It meant, quite simply, that "conviction by means of unlawful seizures and enforced confessions . . . should find no sanction in the judgments of the courts . . ." and that such evidence "shall not be used at all."

In 1949, thirty-five years after *Weeks* was announced, this Court, in *Wolf v. Colorado,* again for the first time, discussed the effect of the Fourth Amendment upon the States through the operation of the Due Process Clause of the Fourteenth Amendment. It said:

"[W]e have no hesitation in saying that were a State affirmatively to sanction such police incursion into privacy it would run counter to the guaranty of the Fourteenth Amendment."

Nevertheless, after declaring that the "security of one's privacy against arbitrary intrusion by the police" is "implicit in 'the concept of ordered liberty' and as such enforceable against the States through the Due Process Clause," and announcing that it "stoutly adhere[d]" to the *Weeks* decision, the Court decided that the Weeks exclusionary rule would not then be imposed upon the States as "an essential ingredient of the right."

While in 1949, prior to the *Wolf* case, almost two-thirds of the States were opposed to the use of the exclusionary rule, now, despite the *Wolf* case, more than half of those since passing upon it, by their own legislative or judicial decision, have wholly or partly adopted or adhered to the *Weeks* rule.

Today we once again examine *Wolf's* constitutional documentation of the right to privacy free from unreasonable State intrusion, and, after its dozen years on our books, are led by it to close the only courtroom door remaining open to evidence secured by official lawlessness in flagrant abuse of the basic right, reserved to all persons as a specific guarantee against that very same unlawful conduct. We hold that all evidence obtained by searches and seizures in violation of the Constitution is, by that same authority, inadmissible in a State court.

Since the Fourth Amendment's right of privacy has been declared enforceable against the States through the Due Process Clause of the Fourteenth, it is enforceable against them by the same sanction of exclusion as is used against the Federal Government. Were it otherwise, then just as without the *Weeks* rule the assurance against unreasonable federal searches and seizures would be "a form of words," valueless and undeserving of mention in a perpetual charter of inestimable human liberties, so too, without that rule the freedom from State invasions of privacy would be so ephemeral and so neatly severed from its conceptual nexus with the freedom from all brutish means of coercing evidence as not to merit this Court's high regard as a freedom "implicit in the concept of ordered liberty."

The ignoble shortcut to conviction left open to the State tends to destroy the entire system of constitutional restraints on which the liberties of the people rest. Having once recognized that the right to privacy embodied in the Fourth Amendment is enforceable against the States, and that the right to be secure against rude invasions of privacy by State officers is, therefore, constitutional in origin, we can no longer permit that right to remain an empty promise. Because it is enforceable in the same manner and to like effect as other basic rights secured by the Due Process Clause, we can no longer permit it to be revocable at the whim of any police officer who, in the name of law enforcement itself, chooses to suspend its enjoyment. Our decision, founded on reason and truth, gives to the individual no more than that which the Constitution guarantees him, to the police officer no less than that to which honest law enforcement is entitled, and, to the courts, that judicial integrity so necessary in the true administration of justice.

IX

PROTECTION AGAINST
DOUBLE JEOPARDY

The compendious Fifth Amendment says that no one shall "for the same offense . . . be twice put in jeopardy of life or limb." This protection applies whether there was an acquittal or a conviction at the first trial.

While this prohibition, like the rest of the Fifth Amendment, is not binding on the States, similar protection is to be found in the constitutions of forty-five of the States. The remaining five States recognize the prohibition against double jeopardy as part of the common law. Its origin is ancient, and it is to be found in Roman law and in European civil law.

But the prohibition against double jeopardy does not prevent State prosecution for conduct for which one has already been punished or acquitted by Federal process if the accused has violated both a State and a Federal penal statute. [*Bartkus v. Illinois;* an abridgment of the Court's opinion is at page 74 and of a dissenting opinion at page 76.] Only one State of the twenty-eight which have considered the problem has ruled against such double prosecution. The double jeopardy prohibition also does not prevent Federal prosecution for the same act if the accused was previously tried in a State court, whether he was there adjudged guilty or acquitted. [*Abbate v. United States,* 359 U.S. 187 (1959); *United States v. Lanza,* 260 U.S. 377 (1922)] But the Attorney General on April 5, 1959 issued a directive to all United States Attorneys that there were to be no federal prosecutions for the same act for which there has been a prior State trial unless the "reasons are compelling" and then only on the specific approval of the Attorney General.

Nor does the Fifth Amendment prohibit prosecution for

violations of several statutes growing out of one act. For example, though a person is tried, convicted, and sentenced for breaking into a post office with the intent to commit larceny, there is no bar against a concurrent or later prosecution for stealing postal funds. The test of identity, which creates a double jeopardy situation, is whether the proof required for conviction is the same. The fact that both charges grow out of one act does not in itself make a single offense where two are defined by statute. [*Morgan v. Devine*, 237 U.S. 632 (1914)]

Because the Supreme Court is not a general court of appeals from the State judicial systems, ordinarily it cannot review a State conviction in which the defendant claims he was tried twice for the same offense. But the Court has taken jurisdiction in extreme cases by establishing, in an appeal from Connecticut, the so-called *Palko Rule*. Palko was tried for murder in the first degree and was found guilty of murder in the second degree. Although in most jurisdictions the State would not have had a right of appeal, under Connecticut law an appeal was properly taken and there was a reversal for errors of law by the trial judge. At a second trial Palko was convicted of first degree murder and sentenced to death, whereupon he appealed to the Supreme Court claiming he had been tried twice for the same offense and that the second trial was unconstitutional under the Fifth Amendment prohibition of double jeopardy. The Court did not sustain his argument, but dictum in the case, subsequently called the *Palko Rule*, is that even though the Federal prohibition of double jeopardy is not binding on the States, where a State's conduct or statute is "so acute and shocking that our polity will not endure it" and is violative of "those fundamental principles of liberty and justice which lie at the base of all our civil and political institutions," then the due process clause of the Fourteenth Amendment intervenes. By this rationale the Court may take jurisdiction where for the same offense one has been tried twice in State courts or where it deems any of the other fundamental essentials of ordered justice denied. [*Palko v. Connecticut;* the Court's opinion, in abridgment, is at page 78.]

BARTKUS v. ILLINOIS, 359 U.S. 121 (1959)

Abridgment of Mr. Justice Frankfurter's Opinion for the Court.

Petitioner was tried in the Federal District Court for the Northern District of Illinois on December 18, 1953, for robbery of a federally insured savings and loan association. . . . The case was tried to a jury and resulted in an acquittal. On January 8, 1954, an Illinois grand jury indicted Bartkus. The facts recited in the Illinois indictment were substantially identical to those contained in the prior federal indictment. The Illinois indictment charged that these facts constituted a violation of Illinois Revised Statutes. . . . Bartkus was tried and convicted in the Criminal Court of Cook County and was sentenced to life imprisonment.

The state and federal prosecutions were separately conducted. It is true that the agent of the Federal Bureau of Investigation who had conducted the investigation on behalf of the Federal Government turned over to the Illinois prosecuting officials all the evidence he had gathered against the petitioner. Concededly, some of that evidence had been gathered after acquittal in the federal court. The only other connection between the two trials is to be found in a suggestion that the federal sentencing of the accomplices who testified against petitioner in both trials was purposely continued by the federal court until after they testified in the state trial. The record establishes that the prosecution was undertaken by state prosecuting officials within their discretionary responsibility and on the basis of evidence that conduct contrary to the penal code of Illinois had occurred within their jurisdiction. It establishes also that federal officials acted in cooperation with state authorities, as is the conventional practice between the two sets of prosecutors throughout the country. It does not support the claim that the State of Illinois in bringing its prosecution was merely a tool of the federal authorities, who thereby avoided the prohibition of the Fifth Amendment against a retrial of a federal prosecution after an acquittal. It does not sustain a conclusion that the state prosecution was a sham and a cover for a federal prosecution, and thereby in essential fact another federal prosecution.

Since the new prosecution was by Illinois, and not by the Federal Government, the claim of unconstitutionality must rest upon the Due Process Clause of the Fourteenth Amendment. We have held from the beginning and uniformly that the Due Process Clause of the Fourteenth Amendment does not apply to the States any of the provisions of the first eight amendments as such.

The experience of state courts in dealing with successive prosecutions by differing governments is obviously . . . relevant in considering whether or not the Illinois prosecution of Bartkus violated due process of law. Of the twenty-eight States which have considered the validity of successive state and federal prosecutions as against a challenge of violation of either a state constitutional double-jeopardy provision or a common-law evidentiary rule of *autrefois acquit and autrefois convict,* twenty-seven have refused to rule that the second prosecution was or would be barred. These States were not bound to follow this Court and its interpretation of the Fifth Amendment. The rules, constitutional, statutory, or common law which bound them, drew upon the same experience as did the Fifth Amendment, but were and are of separate and independent authority.

Not all of the state cases manifest careful reasoning, for in some of them the language concerning double jeopardy is but offhand dictum. But in an array of state cases there may be found full consideration of the arguments supporting and denying a bar to a second prosecution. These courts interpreted their rules as not proscribing a second prosecution where the first was by a different government and for violation of a different statute.

With this body of precedent as irrefutable evidence that state and federal courts have for years refused to bar a second trial even though there had been a prior trial by another government for a similar offense, it would be disregard of a long, unbroken, unquestioned course of impressive adjudication for the Court now to rule that due process compels such a bar.

The entire history of litigation and contention over the question of the imposition of a bar to a second prosecution by a government other than the one first prosecuting is a manifestation of the evolutionary unfolding of law. Today a number of States have statutes which bar a second prosecution if the defendant has been once tried by another government for a similar offense. A study of the cases under the New York statute, which is typical of these laws, demonstrates that the task of determining when the federal and state statutes are so much alike that a prosecution under the former bars a prosecution under the latter is a difficult one. The proper solution of that problem frequently depends upon a judgment of the gravamen of the state statute. It depends also upon an understanding of the scope of the bar that has been historically granted in the State to prevent successive state prosecutions. Both these problems are ones with which the States are obviously more competent to deal than is this Court. Furthermore, the rules resulting will intimately affect the efforts of a State to develop a rational and just body of criminal law in the protection of its citizens. We ought not to utilize the Fourteenth Amendment to interfere with this development. Finally, experience such as that of New York may give aid to Congress in its consideration of adoption of similar provisions in individual federal criminal statutes or in the federal criminal code.

Precedent, experience, and reason alike support the conclusion that Alfonse Bartkus has not been deprived of due process of law by the State of Illinois.

Affirmed

Abridgment of Dissenting Opinion of Mr. Justice Black. (Mr. Justice Brennan dissented in a separate opinion in which Mr. Chief Justice Warren and Mr. Justice Douglas joined.)

Today, for the first time in its history, this Court upholds the state conviction of a defendant who had been *acquitted* of the same offense in the federal courts. I would hold that a federal trial following either state acquittal or conviction is barred by the Double Jeopardy Clause of the Fifth Amendment. And, quite apart from whether that clause is as fully binding on the States as it is on the Federal Government, . . . I would hold that Bartkus' conviction cannot stand. For I think double prosecutions for the same offense are so contrary to the spirit of our free country that they violate even the prevailing view of the Fourteenth Amendment, expressed in *Palko v. Connecticut.* . . .

Fear and abhorrence of governmental power to try people twice for the same conduct is one of the oldest ideas found in western civilization. Its roots run deep into Greek and Roman times. Even in the Dark Ages, when so many other principles of justice were lost, the idea that one trial and one punishment were enough remained alive through the canon law and the teachings of the early Christian writers. By the thirteenth century it seems to have been firmly established in England, where it came to be considered as a "universal maxim of the common law." It is not surprising, therefore, that the principle was brought to this country by the earliest settlers as part of their heritage of freedom, and that it has been recognized here as fundamental again and again. Today it is found, in varying forms, not only in the Federal Constitution, but in the jurisprudence or constitutions of every State, as well as most foreign nations. Few principles have been more deeply "rooted in the traditions and conscience of our people."

The Court apparently takes the position that a second trial for the same act is somehow less offensive if one of the trials is conducted by the Federal Government and the other by a State. Looked at from the standpoint of the individual who is being prosecuted, this notion is too subtle for me to grasp. If double punishment is what is feared, it hurts no less for two "Sovereigns" to inflict it than for one. If danger to the innocent is emphasized, that danger is surely no less when the power of the State and Federal Governments is brought to bear on one man in two trials, than when one of these "Sovereigns" proceeds alone. In each case, inescapably, a man is forced to face danger twice for the same conduct.

There are some countries that allow the dangerous practice of trying people twice. I had thought that our constitutional protections embodied in the Double Jeopardy and Due Process Clauses would have barred any such things happening here. Unfortunately, last year's holdings by this Court in *Ciucci v. Illinois* . . . and *Hoag v. New Jersey,* . . . and today's affirmance of the convictions of Bartkus and Abbate cause me to fear that in an important number of cases it can happen here.

I would reverse.

PALKO v. CONNECTICUT, 302 U.S. 319 (1937)

Abridgment of Mr. Justice Cardozo's Opinion for the Court.

The argument for appellant is that whatever is forbidden by the Fifth Amendment is forbidden by the Fourteenth also. The Fifth Amendment, which is not directed to the states, but solely to the federal government, creates immunity from double jeopardy.

Right-minded men . . . could reasonably, even if mistakenly, believe that a second trial was lawful in prosecutions subject to the Fifth Amendment, if it was all in the same case. Even more plainly, right-minded men could reasonably believe that in espousing that conclusion they were not favoring a practice repugnant to the conscience of mankind. Is double jeopardy in such circumstances, if double jeopardy it must be called, a denial of due process forbidden to the states? The tyranny of labels . . . must not lead us to leap to a conclusion that a word which in one set of facts may stand for oppression or enormity is of like effect in every other.

We have said that in appellant's view the Fourteenth Amendment is to be taken as embodying the prohibitions of the Fifth. His thesis is even broader. Whatever would be a violation of the original bill of rights (Amendments I to VIII) if done by the federal government is now equally unlawful by force of the Fourteenth Amendment if done by a state. There is no such general rule.

The Fifth Amendment provides, among other things, that no person shall be held to answer for a capital or otherwise infamous crime unless on presentment or indictment of a grand jury. This court has held that, in prosecutions by a state, presentment or indictment by a grand jury may give way to informations at the instance of a public officer. The Fifth Amendment provides also that no person shall be compelled in any criminal case to be a witness against himself. This court has said that, in prosecutions by a state, the exemption will fail if the state elects to end it. The Sixth Amendment calls for a jury trial in criminal cases and the Seventh for a jury trial in civil cases at common law where the value in controversy shall exceed twenty dollars. This court has ruled that consistently with those amendments trial by jury may be modified by a state or abolished altogether.

On the other hand, the due process clause of the Fourteenth Amendment may make it unlawful for a state to abridge by its statutes the freedom of speech which the First Amendment safeguards against encroachment by the Congress . . . or the like freedom of the press, . . . or the free exercise of religion, . . . or the right of peaceable assembly, without which speech would be unduly trammeled, . . . or the right of one accused of crime to the benefit of counsel. . . . In these and other situations immunities that are valid as against the federal government by force of the specific pledges of particular amendments have been found to be implicit in the concept of ordered liberty, and thus, through the Fourteenth Amendment, become valid as against the states.

The line of division may seem to be wavering and broken if there is a hasty catalogue of the cases on the one side and the other. Reflection and analysis will induce a different view. There emerges the perception of a rationalizing principle which gives to discrete instances a proper order and coherence. The right to trial by jury and the immunity from prosecution except as the result of an indictment may have value and importance. Even so, they are not of the very essence of a scheme of ordered liberty. To abolish them is not to violate a "principle of justice so rooted in the traditions and conscience of our people as to be ranked as fundamental." Few would be so narrow or provincial as to maintain that a fair and enlightened system of justice would be impossible without them. What is true of jury trials and indictments is true also, as the cases show, of the immunity from compulsory self-incrimination.

We reach a different plane of social and moral values when we pass to the privileges and immunities that have been taken over from the earlier articles of the federal bill of rights and brought within the Fourteenth Amendment by a process of absorption. These in their origin were effective against the federal government alone. If the Fourteenth Amendment has absorbed them, the process of absorption has had its source in the belief that neither liberty nor justice would exist if they were sacrificed. This is true, for illustration, of freedom of thought, and speech. Fundamental too in the concept of due process, and so in that of liberty, is the thought that condemnation shall be rendered only after trial. The hearing, moreover, must be a real one, not a sham or a pretense. For that reason, ignorant defendants in a capital case were held to have been condemned unlawfully when in truth, though not in form, they were refused the aid of counsel. The decision did not turn upon the fact that the benefit of counsel would have been guaranteed to the defendants by the provisions of the Sixth Amendment if they had been prosecuted in a federal court. The decision turned upon the fact that in the particular situation laid before us in the evidence the benefit of counsel was essential to the substance of a hearing.

On which side of the line the case made out by the appellant has appropriate location must be the next inquiry and the final one. Is that kind of double jeopardy to which the statute has subjected him a hardship so acute and shocking that our polity will not endure it? Does it violate those "fundamental principles of liberty and justice which lie at the base of all our civil and political institutions"? The answer surely must be "no." The state is not attempting to wear the accused out by a multitude of cases with accumulated trials. It asks no more than this, that the case against him shall go on until there shall be a trial free from the corrosion of substantial legal error. This is not cruelty at all, nor even vexation in any immoderate degree.

The judgment is Affirmed.

X

THE RIGHT TO HAVE BAIL AND THE PROTECTION AGAINST CRUEL AND UNUSUAL PUNISHMENT

The Eighth Amendment contains two prohibitions applicable to penal matters: it says that "excessive bail shall not be required, . . . nor cruel and unusual punishments inflicted."

It is important that one accused of crime be admitted to reasonable bail. Otherwise, the innocent would be imprisoned while awaiting trial, and the accused would be handicapped in consulting counsel, in searching for evidence and witnesses, and in preparing for trial or appeal. True, admitting an accused person to bail carries with it the danger that he may flee and not be available for trial or sentence, but this is a calculated risk that society must take as the price of a proper system of justice. The Federal Rules of Criminal Procedure provide that all persons arrested for a noncapital offense be admitted to bail.

But if a court fixes bail in an excessive amount, the effect is a complete denial of bail.

The reported cases of excessive bail are not ordinarily for crimes of violence but are almost invariably cases involving unpopular causes. Some are odd cases that arose under the former Prohibition law, and more recently there were several security cases and cases involving the civil rights struggle in the South. The appellate courts have almost uniformly lowered bail where a trial court fixed it at an unreasonably high amount.

While no mathematical formula can be used to determine the proper bail, the facts in each case are to be tested against the Federal Rules of Criminal Procedure, which provide that the amount of bail shall be sufficient to insure the presence of the defendant, having regard to the nature and circumstances of the offense, the weight of the evidence against the accused, his financial ability to give bail, and his character.

Supreme Court Justice Jackson, made a statement concerning the right to reasonable bail which is applicable as a general rule to any constitutional problem:

> But the right of every American to equal treatment before the law is wrapped up in the same constitutional bundle. . . . If in anger . . . with these defendants we throw out the bundle, we also cast aside protection for . . . [all]. [*Williamson v. United States;* the Court's opinion, in abridgment, is at page 85.]

While the State courts have had a number of cases in which prison sentences were held to be excessive, the Supreme Court has had only three cases in which it was asked to determine that punishment was cruel and unusual. The first appeal came to the Court from the Philippine Islands in 1910 before the Philippines received their independence. For making a false entry of 616 pesos in public records, the defendant was fined 4,000 pesos and sentenced to twelve years in prison, with additional punishments such as wearing chains and a perpetual loss of his civil rights. The Supreme Court held this punishment to be cruel and unusual when tested against the limitations of both the Eighth Amendment and a similar provision in the Philippine Bill of Rights. The appellant was discharged from custody. [*Weems v. United States,* 217 U.S. 349]

The Court made the significant statement that the Eighth Amendment is progressive, and that punishment is to be considered in the light of today's society. This view is in accord with the general recognition that the Court has given to the Constitution and the Amendments as dynamic and not static. Benjamin N. Cardozo, later a Supreme Court Justice, in the 1921 William L. Storrs Lectures at Yale University, speaking of "The Judge as a Legislator," stated this outlook: "Law is, indeed, an historical growth, for it is an expression of customary morality which develops silently and unconsciously from one age to another." [*The Nature of the Judicial Process,* Yale University Press (1921)]

The Court had its second case on cruel and unusual punishment in 1947. The petitioner was duly convicted in the Louisiana state courts of murder and sentenced to be electrocuted. In accordance with the warrant and with all the legal requirements as to witnesses and other formalities, he was placed in the electric chair. The switch was thrown by the executioner but, because of some mechanical difficulty, death did not result even though some electricity passed through the prisoner. The Supreme Court, by a five to four decision, denied the appellant's claim that to subject him to a second attempt at execution was cruel and unusual punishment when tested against the Eighth Amendment. The holding of the Court was that while the prisoner was subjected to unusual pain and suffering, it was because of an accident for which the State was not responsible. The dissenting Justices argued vehemently that the second electrocution should be prohibited, that it was as unthinkable to approve a law which permitted execution in slow stages as it would be to countenance one that expressly provided for such an execution. [*Louisiana v. Resweber*, 329 U.S. 459 (1947)]

Reading the Court's and the dissenting opinions in *Resweber* (the Louisiana case) together with the holding in *Weems* (the Philippine case), it is clear that *Resweber* does not establish a rule except perhaps for the identical facts that were before the Court then, and that the prevailing interpretation of what constitutes cruel and unusual punishment is the earlier *Weems* case.

A different type of punishment is involved in the case of one Trop, a native born American, who was denied a passport on the grounds that he had lost his citizenship by reason of his conviction and dishonorable discharge for desertion from the armed forces during wartime. The question *Trop* presented to the Court was whether denationalization may be used as a punishment as distinguished from the accepted practice of cancelling citizenship for fraud in the application for naturalization. Previously, the Court had held that citizenship may be forfeited by an affirmative act such as voting in a foreign election. Starting from the premise that fines, imprisonment, and even execution may be imposed depending on the enormity of the offense, the Court held:

. . . the use of denationalization as a punishment is barred by the Eighth Amendment. . . . It is a form of punishment more primitive than torture for it destroys for the individual the political existence that was centuries in the development. The punishment strips the citizen of his status in the national and international community. His very existence is at the suffrance of the country in which he happens to find himself. . . .

This punishment is offensive to cardinal principles for which the Constitution stands. It subjects the individual to a fate of ever-increasing fear and distress. . . . It is no answer to suggest that all the disastrous consequences of this fate may not be brought to bear on a stateless person. The threat makes the punishment obnoxious. [*Trop v. Dulles,* 356 U.S. 86 (1958)]

In many primitive societies banishment was the penalty for the most extreme offenses. It was harsher punishment than a death sentence. The offender became a stateless person, wandering in constant terror as a stranger in foreign territory, the prey of wild animals and any person he met. The Court may well have been thinking of this mark of Cain when it declared Trop a citizen.

WILLIAMSON v. UNITED STATES, 184 F.2d. 280 (1950)

Abridgment of the Opinion of Mr. Justice Jackson sitting as Circuit Justice for the Second Circuit.

These Communist Party leaders were convicted for conspiring to advocate and teach the violent overthrow of the United States Government and to organize the Communist Party for that purpose. They were not charged with any attempt or with any overt act toward that end other than those incident to such organization and teaching.

Defendants appealed and, after denial of bail by the trial court, applied to the Court of Appeals for its allowance. Government counsel conceded that the appeal presented a substantial question and upon that concession defendants were enlarged upon bond.

After the Court of Appeals affirmed the convictions, defendants expressed an intention to petition the Supreme Court to review their cases. The prosecution asked that bail be revoked and defendants remanded to jail. Two grounds were advanced: first, that no substantial question as to the validity of the conviction survived the affirmance, and second, that defendants, while at large, *have pursued* and *will continue to pursue* a course of conduct and activity dangerous to the public welfare, safety and national security of the United States. The Court of Appeals did not summarily terminate bail but a majority of the judges extended it for thirty days, expressly to enable application to the Circuit Justice for further extension. Chief Judge Hand, who had written the principal opinion affirming the convictions, said he regarded the case as "involving substantial questions and therefore entitling the defendants to remain on bail pending certiorari."

To remain at large, under bond, after conviction and until the courts complete the process of settling substantial questions which underlie the determination of guilt cannot be demanded as a matter of right. It rests in sound judicial discretion. Only in a rare case will I override a clear and direct decision by the Court of Appeals that bail ought to be granted or denied. But here one judge favored its allowance, and the action of his two associates in granting a thirty–day extension implied the continuing power to grant bail, which is dependent on persistence of a substantial question and indicated that they did not regard the defendants as presenting a very immediate public danger.

I cannot accept the Government's first contention that no substantial question survives for Supreme Court review.

The Government's alternative contention is that defendants, by misbehavior after conviction, have forfeited their claim to bail. Grave public danger is said to result from what they may be expected to do, in addition to what they have done since their conviction. If I assume that defendants are disposed to commit every opportune disloyal act helpful to Communist countries, it is still difficult to reconcile with traditional American law the jailing of persons by the courts because of anticipated but as yet uncommitted crimes. Imprisonment to protect society from predicted but unconsummated offenses is so unprecedented in this country and so fraught with danger of excesses and injustice that I am loath to resort to it, even as a discretionary judicial technique to supplement conviction of such offenses as those of which defendants stand convicted.

Turning then to past, but post-conviction, activities said to be dangerous, I find them to consist entirely of making speeches and writing articles or editorials, chiefly for the Communist Party organ the Daily Worker. They do not contain any advocacy of violent overthrow of the Government and can only be said to be inciting, as all opposition speaking or writing that undermines confidence and increases discontent may be said to be incitement. These, however, are severely critical of the policy of the United States toward Korea and favorable to the Soviet position. Some are crudely intemperate, contain falsehoods obvious to the informed, and all are plainly designed to embroil different elements of our society and embarrass those who are presently conducting the Government. But the very essence of constitutional freedom of press and of speech is to allow more liberty than the good citizen will take. The test of its vitality is whether we will suffer and protect much that we think false, mischievous and bad, both in taste and intent.

It is not contended that these utterances, in themselves, are criminal. The Communist Party has not been outlawed either by legislation, nor by these convictions, and its right to publish the Daily Worker is not questioned. Nor were defendants indicted under that part of the statute which prohibits publication of matter intended to cause overthrow and destruction of government. Since the paper may lawfully be issued, certainly its publishers or contributors may comment critically on the Government's conduct of foreign affairs. If the Government cannot get at these utterances by direct prosecution, it is hard to see how courts can justifiably reach and stop them by indirection.

It is said, however, that freedoms of speech or press cannot be invoked by defendants because their speeches and publications constitute a repetition of their offenses and a continuation of the conspiracy of which they have been convicted. If all that convicted these defendants was such utterances as have followed their conviction, there would indeed be doubt about its validity, for I am unable to find in them any word of advocacy of violence either to overthrow the Government or of forcible resistance to its policy.

My task would be simple if a judge were free to order persons imprisoned because he thinks their opinions are obnoxious, their motives evil and that free society would be bettered by their absence. The plea of admitted Communist leaders for liberties and rights here, which they deny to all persons wherever they have seized power, is so hypocritical that it can fairly and dispassionately be judged only with effort.

But the right of every American to equal treatment before the law is wrapped up in the same constitutional bundle with those of these Communists. If in anger or disgust with these defendants we throw out the bundle, we also cast aside protection for the liberties of more worthy critics who may be in opposition to the government of some future day.

If, however, I were to be wrong on all of these abstract or theoretical matters of principle, there is a very practical aspect of this application which must not be overlooked or underestimated—that is the disastrous effect on the reputation of American justice if I should now send these men to jail and the full Court later decide that their conviction is invalid. Under no circumstances must we permit their symbolization of an evil force in the world to be hallowed and glorified by any semblance of martyrdom. The way to avoid that risk is not to jail these men until it is finally decided that they should stay jailed.

Their bail as fixed by the Court of Appeals is therefore continued until the Supreme Court of the United States shall deny their petition for certiorari or, if it be granted, shall render judgment upon their cause.

XI

FREEDOM OF SPEECH AND OF THE PRESS: THE DOCTRINE OF "CLEAR AND PRESENT DANGER"

The First Amendment charges Congress ". . . to make no law . . . abridging the freedom of speech or of the press." At the time of the adoption of the Bill of Rights, there was little discussion as to what was meant by freedom of speech. As it was a freedom unanimously desired, there was no controversial debate defining it. Definition was a task left to later Congresses and the courts.

The right to speak with freedom is put to its strongest test when the privilege is claimed by one who holds ideas politically or economically in opposition to the majority. But not to grant liberty of expression to one with whom one violently disagrees is to deny freedom to all.

Early in the life of the Republic, the Federalist Party, which was then in power and consisted chiefly of the landed gentry and rich merchants, feared Thomas Jefferson and his newly organized Republican Party. The Federalists attempted to silence the Republicans' appeal to the masses by passing the Alien and Sedition Acts of 1798. (This Republican Party is not today's Republican Party.)

The Alien Act authorized the President to order the deportation, without trial or hearing, of any alien whom he judged to be "dangerous to the peace and safety of the United States." The Act was never invoked and it expired, by its terms, in two years but because of its threat a number of aliens, including several newspapers editors, left the country and others gave up all public activity.

The Sedition Act made a crime of almost any criticism of the President, Congress, or the government. The offense was ". . . to excite against [the President, Congress, or the Federal government] the hatred of the good people of the United States." There were some fifteen prosecutions, and even more arrests, under it. The first of the prosecutions was against Mathew Lyon, a Republican Congressman from Vermont. His offense was to publish an article attacking the administration, charging that "every consideration of the public welfare was swallowed up in a continual grasp for power, in an unbounded thirst for public pomp, foolish adulation, and selfish avarice" and to publish a letter from Joel Barlow, an American poet and political essayist then in France, which urged Congress to commit President Adams to an asylum for the insane. Lyon was convicted, fined, and sentenced to jail. While in prison he was re-elected to Congress by Republican Vermont.

The Sedition Act's complete negation of freedom of speech threw the country in a turmoil. In the 1800 election the Federalists were voted out of power and Jefferson was elected President. The Sedition Act expired on March 3, 1801. Jefferson pardoned all who had been convicted under the Act, dismissed the cases awaiting trial, and Congress repaid most of the fines. Jefferson said:

> I discharged every person under punishment or prosecution under the Sedition law, because I considered and now consider that law to be a nullity, as absolute and as palpable as if Congress had ordered us to fall down and worship a golden image.

For the next hundred years, little thought was given to freedom of speech. It was an assumed right and broadly exercised without any legislation either propounding or restricting it. True, during the Civil War there were many arrests for sedition, but this was a time of actual rebellion and civil war. And the prosecutions, though numerous, were of such a nature that they did not prevent vituperative criticism of candidates in an election held in the midst of the war.

It was not until the First World War that concepts arose holding that speech was not entirely free. But a Sedition Act passed in 1918 was repealed, three years after its adoption, although in the interim there were many hundreds of prosecutions for the expression of unpopular opinion. There were convictions for making statements to the effect that all war was immoral and un-Christian and for urging heavier taxation in place of bond issues.

While the people and the courts of the United States had approached the World War I period with no statutory or judicial definition of the meaning of the First Amendment guarantee of freedom of expression, there was in the history and culture of the country a profound respect for the right to speak and write without restraint. The colonies in good part were founded by men who had fled England because of religious persecution. And the right to practice one's own religion is parallel to the right to speak freely on secular matters. It is understandable that both these freedoms were put in the same section of the Bill of Rights.

Some forty years before the Revolution, the colonies were shaken by the trial of Peter Zenger, who was charged with sedition because, in the *New York Weekly Journal* of which he was editor, he criticized the colonial governor. Zenger had published the statement:

> We see judges arbitrarily displaced, new courts erected without consent of the legislature, trials by jury taken away when a governor pleases. Who . . . then [may] call any thing his own, or enjoy any liberty longer than those in the Administration will condescend to let them do it? For this reason I have left [New York] as I believe more will.

While in prison for nearly a year awaiting trial, Zenger continued to publish the *Journal*. He was well served here by the English common law which had abolished prior restraint, that is, the suppression of a writing before its publication, The Zenger trial aroused tremendous interest in all the colonies. Indeed, its proceedings were reported throughout the world.

The Sedition Act under which Zenger was charged made criticism of the government a crime. Zenger's lawyer, Andrew Hamilton, who came out of retirement for this case, based his plea to the jury on the necessity of free speech if men were to be free of political tyranny. Zenger was acquitted by the jury, and throughout the colonies there was rejoicing. The spirit that this trial evoked was substantially responsible for the inclusion of freedom of speech in the First Amendment. And, indeed the incorporation of First Amendment rights in the constitutional restriction of the States by the Fourteenth Amendment is part of this heritage.

It was the World War I attack on freedom of speech and the press, based on the Sedition Act of 1918 and various State laws, that started the flood of appeals to the United States Supreme Court which continues to this day. Very little has been or can be done toward establishing a general rule. Each case has been determined on its own facts and in relation to its time.

The eighteenth century Virginia Bill for Establishing Religious Freedom spelled out instructions that might well have been followed as the ultimate test as to when speech may lawfully be inhibited. It said: ". . . it is time enough for the rightful purposes of civil government, for its officers to interfere when principles break out into overt acts against peace and good order."

Under the Espionage Act of 1917 (of which the Sedition Act of 1918 was a part), Schenck, the secretary of the Socialist Party, was found guilty of conspiracy to cause insubordination in the armed forces and to obstruct recruiting by publishing a circular attacking conscription. Schenck asked the Supreme Court to reverse his conviction, claiming that it was an infringement of his right to free speech under the First Amendment. Justice Holmes, substantially though not entirely following the reasoning that inspired the differentiation between "overt acts" and speech in the 1785 Virginia Statute, said:

> We admit that in many places and in ordinary times the defendants in saying all that was said in the circular would have been within their constitutional rights. But the character of every act depends upon the circumstances in which it is done. . . . The most stringent protection of free speech would not protect a man in falsely shouting fire in a theatre and causing a panic. . . . The question in every case is whether the words used are used in such

circumstances and are of such nature as to create a clear and present danger that they will bring about the substantive evils that Congress has a right to prevent. It is a question of proximity and degree. When a nation is at war many things that might be said in time of peace are such a hindrance to its effort that their utterance will not be endured so long as men fight, and that no Court could regard them as protected by any constitutional right. [*Schenck v. United States* 249 U.S. 47 (1919)]

The phrase "clear and present danger" was expanded into a doctrine that received increasing acceptance. It was a sound and useful tool in judicial determination of the conflict of interests of the fundamental freedoms of speech, press, and religion when opposed to the security or welfare of the country. But after a life of vicissitude and yet growth from its beginning in World War I, the doctrine received a crippling and well nigh mortal blow in the period following World War II when the leaders of the Communist Party appealed from their conviction for advocating the overthrow of the government. The charge against them under the Smith Act of 1940 was not attempting to overthrow the government, but organizing the Communist Party for the purpose of *advocating* the government's overthrow.

In the affirmance of the convictions in this case [*Dennis v. United States,* 341 U.S. 494 (1951)], the court used language of respect for the "clear and present danger" doctrine but so emasculated it that it survived as mere verbiage and not a rule of law. When Holmes and Brandeis wrote of "clear and present danger," they distinguished between action and exhortation, and even when there was action, required that it be substantive. Advocacy of violence, if it fell short of incitement for immediate action to cause a "relatively serious evil" and not a "trivial harm" created a conflict of interest to be resolved in favor of the right to speak: "The fact that speech is likely to result in some violence or destruction of property is not enough to justify its suppression." But they also found justification to suppress speech when there was "*actual probability*" of serious injury to the state." This condition seriously qualified the forthright Jeffersonian requirement, as set out in the Virginia Act for Religious Freedom, that until speech developed into *"overt acts,"* it was to be free and unrestricted.

In the *Dennis* case, the doctrine of "present danger" gave way to "probable danger" in some distant future. Judge Learned Hand, who wrote the opinion in the Court of Appeals (which the Supreme Court followed), overlooked the established American philosophy that if there were no "present danger," then speech should be free since time would intervene during which the truth could prevail. He disregarded Brandeis's injunction: "If there be time to expose through discussion the falsehood and fallacies, to avert the evil by the processes of education, the remedy to be applied is more speech, not enforced silence." [*Whitney v. California;* the Court's opinion, in abridgment, is at page 97.]

The prevailing doubt as to whether local leaders or members generally of the Communist Party are subject to prosecution under the Smith Act was finally resolved by the Court in the *Scales* case by a five-to-four affirmance; they are so subject. Junius Scales was first convicted in 1955; after hearing his appeal in 1956 the Court asked for re-argument the following year. It reversed, ordering a new trial because of procedural defects. At this second trial, Scales was again convicted. The Court heard argument on his appeal in 1959, ordered re-argument in 1960 and affirmed the conviction in 1961. This decision is a determination that a Smith Act conviction of an "active" though not a "nominal or passive Communist Party member" is not violative of constitutional protection or immunity. [*Scales v. United States,* 366 U.S. 978 (1961)]

At the same time the Court unanimously reversed another conviction under the Smith Act membership clause, holding that in this case the proof was insufficient to establish illegal advocacy by the Communist Party of the violent overthrow of the Government. Justice Harlan's opinion for the majority said:

> We held [in *Yates* in 1957] and we reiterate now that the mere abstract teaching of Communist theory, including the teaching of the moral propriety or even moral necessity for a resort to force and violence is not the same as preparing a group for violent action and steeling it to such action. [*Noto v. United States,* 367 U.S. 290 (1961]

The Internal Security Act of 1950 requires "Communist-action" and "Communist-front" organizations to register with the Government. The law defines a Communist-action group as one that is "substantially directed" by a foreign government "controlling the world Communist movement." A Communist-front organization is defined as one "substantially controlled by a Communist-action" organization. The required registration includes listing all officers and members within the past year and a statement of the source of all income and itemization of all expenses for the year. Upon registration, the organization loses any tax exemption it may have, it is required to endorse its mail "Disseminated by [the name of the organization], a Communist organization." The members are barred from Federal employment, they may not secure or use a passport, and naturalized citizens who join the organization within five years of their naturalization may lose their citizenship.

A 1953 decision of the Subversive Activities Control Board that the Communist Party was controlled by a foreign government was set aside by the Court on the grounds that the Board had based its decision on evidence from proven perjurers. After a second order of the Board was set aside by the Court of Appeals, the Board in 1959 entered a third order that the Communist Party must register. This the Court affirmed on June 5, 1961 with four Justices dissenting in whole or in part. Justice Black alone considered the entire Act in its relationship to the Constitution, finding it a violation of First Amendment rights, a bill of attainder, and a denial of due process, saying:

> The first banning of an association because it advocates hated ideas—whether that association be called a political party or not—marks a fateful moment in the history of a free country. That moment seems to have arrived for this country.

The majority opinion written by Justice Frankfurter, in addition to upholding the requirement to register, held that the names of officers and members and a financial accounting must be filed. But it did not pass on the constitutionality of the requirement that Party officers sign a statement which might be in contradiction of the Fifth Amendment immunity against self incrimination. The Court also refused, as unnecessary at the time, to pass on the penalties that follow registration, that is, the requirement to endorse all mail, the loss of tax exemption, and the deprivation of members' rights to passports. The majority opinion of Justice Frankfurter said:

> When existing government is menaced by a worldwide integrated movement which employs every combination of possible means, peaceful and violent, domestic and foreign, overt and clandestine, to destroy the Government itself—the legislative judgment as to how that threat may best be met consistently with the safeguarding of personal freedom is not to be set aside merely because the judgment of judges would, in the first instance, have chosen other methods. [*Communist Party v. Subversive Activities Control Board*, 367 U.S. 1 (1961)]

Freedom of speech was a right often in contention in connection with activities of the House Committee on Un-American Activities. This Committee was shorn of much of its prestige when the Court in 1957, reversing the *Watkins* conviction for contempt for refusing to testify before the Committee, held that under the due process clause and the First Amendment Watkins was not required to answer the Committee's exploratory questions and that the Committee must show that its inquiry was pertinent to its function of securing data for future lawmaking. Chief Justice Warren speaking for the Court, with only Justice Clark dissenting, said: "An excessively broad charter, like that of the House Un-American Activities Committee, places the courts in an untenable position if they are to strike a balance between the public need for a particular interrogation and the right of citizens to carry on their affairs free from unnecessary interference." [*Watkins v. United States*, 354 U.S. 178 (1957)]

Two years later, though, in 1959, with two new Justices on the Court, and Justices Frankfurter and Harlan abandoning the position they took in *Watkins*, the Court in the *Barenblatt* case gave the House Un-American Activities Committee judicial approval, almost completely negating the effect of the *Watkins* case.

Lloyd Barenblatt, a former Vassar College instructor, had

refused to answer questions of the House Un-American Activities Committee about Communist associations, saying that the Committee's only purpose was "exposure for exposure's sake" and that it violated his right to freedom of speech and association. The Supreme Court upheld his contempt conviction, referring to Congressional findings that communism seeks the overthrow of the Government and that the Court had ". . . consistently refused to view the Communist party as an ordinary political party." Justice Black, in a vigorous dissenting opinion in which he was joined by Chief Justice Warren and Justice Douglas, said:

> Ultimately, all the questions in this case really boil down to one—whether we as a people will try fearfully and futilely to preserve democracy by adopting totalitarian methods, or whether in accordance with our traditions and our Constitution we will have the confidence and courage to be free. [*Barenblatt v. United States;* the dissenting opinion, in abridgment, is at page 100.]

WHITNEY v. CALIFORNIA, 274 U.S. 357 (1927)

Abridgment of Concurring Opinion of Mr. Justice Brandeis. (Mr. Justice Sanford wrote the Opinion for the Court.)

Miss Whitney was convicted of the felony of assisting in organizing, in the year 1919, the Communist Labor Party of California, of being a member of it, and of assembling with it. These acts are held to constitute a crime, because the party was formed to teach criminal syndicalism. The statute which made these acts a crime restricted the right of free speech and of assembly theretofore existing. The claim is that the statute, as applied, denied to Miss Whitney the liberty guaranteed by the Fourteenth Amendment.

The felony which the statute created is a crime very unlike the old felony of conspiracy or the old misdemeanor of unlawful assembly. The mere act of assisting in forming a society for teaching syndicalism, of becoming a member of it, or of assembling with others for that purpose is given the dynamic quality of crime. There is guilt although the society may not contemplate immediate promulgation of the doctrine. Thus the accused is to be punished, not for contempt, incitement or conspiracy, but for a step in preparation, which, if it threatens the public order at all, does so only remotely. The novelty in the prohibition introduced is that the statute aims, not at the practice of criminal syndicalism, nor even directly at the preaching of it, but at association with those who propose to preach it.

[A]lthough the rights of free speech and assembly are fundamental, they are not in their nature absolute. Their exercise is subject to restriction, if the particular restriction proposed is required in order to protect the State from destruction or from serious injury, political, economic or moral. That the necessity which is essential to a valid restriction does not exist unless speech would produce, or is intended to produce, a clear and imminent danger of some substantive evil which the State constitutionally may seek to prevent has been settled.

The legislature must obviously decide, in the first instance, whether a danger exists which calls for a particular protective measure. But where a statute is valid only in case certain conditions exist, the enactment of the statute cannot alone establish the facts which are essential to its validity.

This Court has not yet fixed the standard by which to determine when a danger shall be deemed clear; how remote the danger may be and yet be deemed present; and what degree of evil shall be deemed sufficiently substantial to justify resort to abridgment of free speech and assembly as the means of protection.

Fear of serious injury cannot alone justify suppression of free speech and assembly. Men feared witches and burnt women. It is the function of speech to free men from the bondage of irrational fears. To justify suppression of free speech there must be reasonable ground to fear that serious evil will result if free speech is practiced. The wide difference between advocacy and incitement, between preparation and attempt, between assembling and conspiracy, must be borne in mind. In order to support a finding of clear and present danger it must be shown either that immediate serious violence was to be expected or was advocated, or that the past conduct furnished reason to believe that such advocacy was then contemplated.

To courageous, self-reliant men, with confidence in the power of free and fearless reasoning applied through the processes of popular government, no danger flowing from speech can be deemed clear and present, unless the incidence of the evil apprehended is so imminent that it may befall before there is opportunity for full discussion. If there be time to expose through discussion the falsehood and fallacies, to avert the evil by the processes of education, the remedy to be applied is more speech, not enforced silence. Only an emergency can justify repression. Such must be the rule if authority is to be reconciled with freedom.

Whether in 1919, when Miss Whitney did the things complained of, there was in California such clear and present danger of serious evil, might have been made the important issue in the case. She might have required that the issue be determined either by the court or the jury. She claimed below that the statute as applied to her violated the Federal Constitution; but she did not claim that it was void because there was no clear and present danger of serious evil, nor did she request that the existence of these conditions of a valid measure thus restricting the rights of free speech and assembly be passed upon by the court or a jury. On the other hand, there was evidence on which the court or jury might have found that such danger existed. I am unable to assent to the suggestion in the opinion of the Court that assembling with a political party, formed to advocate the desirability of a proletarian revolution by mass action at some date necessarily far in the future, is not a right within the protection of the Fourteenth Amendment. In the present case, however, there was other testimony which tended to establish the existence of a conspiracy, on the part of members of the International Workers of the World, to commit present serious crimes; and likewise to show that such a conspiracy would be furthered by the activity of the society of which Miss Whitney was a member. Under these circumstances the judgment of the state court cannot be disturbed.

BARENBLATT v. UNITED STATES, 360 U.S. 109 (1959)

Abridgment of Dissenting Opinion of Mr. Justice Black with whom Mr. Chief Justice Warren and Mr. Justice Douglas concurred. (Mr. Justice Brennan concurred in a separate opinion.)

On May 28, 1954, petitioner Lloyd Barenblatt, then . . . a teacher of psychology at Vassar College, was summoned to appear before a Subcommittee of the House Committee on Un-American Activities. After service of the summons, but before Barenblatt appeared . . . , his four-year contract with Vassar expired and was not renewed. He, therefore, came to the Committee as a private citizen without a job. Barenblatt, however, refused to answer their questions and filed a long statement outlining his constitutional objections. He argued that however he answered questions relating to membership in the Communist Party his position in society and his ability to earn a living would be seriously jeopardized; that he would, in effect, be subjected to a bill of attainder despite the twice-expressed constitutional mandate against such legislative punishments.

It goes without saying that a law to be valid must be clear enough to make its commands understandable. For obvious reasons, the standard of certainty required in criminal statutes is more exacting than in noncriminal statutes. This Court has recognized that the stricter standard is as much required in criminal contempt cases as in all other criminal cases. . . . Vagueness becomes even more intolerable in this area if one accepts, as the Court today does, a balancing test to decide if First Amendment rights shall be protected. It is difficult at best to make a man guess—at the penalty of imprisonment—whether a court will consider the State's need for certain information superior to society's interest in unfettered freedom. It is unconscionable to make him choose between the right to keep silent and the need to speak when the statute supposedly establishing the "state's interest" is too vague to give him guidance.

Measured by the foregoing standards, Rule XI [of the House of Representatives] cannot support any conviction for refusal to testify. In substance it authorizes the Committee to compel witnesses to give evidence about all "un-American propaganda," whether instigated in this country or abroad. The word "propaganda" seems to mean anything that people say, write, think or associate together about. The term "un-American" is equally vague.

If Congress wants ideas investigated, if it even wants them investigated in the field of education, it must be prepared to say so expressly and unequivocally. And it is not enough that a court through exhaustive research can establish, even conclusively, that Congress wished to allow the investigation. I can find no such unequivocal statement here.

I do not agree that laws directly abridging First Amendment freedoms can be justified by a congressional or judicial balancing process.

But even assuming what I cannot assume, that some balancing is proper in this case, I feel that the Court after stating the test ignores it completely. At most it balances the right of the Government to preserve itself, against Barenblatt's right to refrain from revealing Communist affiliations. Such a balance, however, mistakes the factors to be weighed. In the first place, it completely leaves out the real interest in Barenblatt's silence, the interest of the people as a whole in being able to join organizations, advocate causes and make political "mistakes" without later being subjected to governmental penalties for having dared to think for themselves. It is this right, the right to err politically, which keeps us strong as a Nation. [T]he obloquy which results from investigations such as this not only stifles "mistakes" but prevents all but the most courageous from hazarding any views which might at some later time become disfavored. This result, whose importance cannot be overestimated, is doubly crucial when it affects the universities, on which we must largely rely for the experimentation and development of new ideas essential to our country's welfare. It is these interests of society, rather than Barenblatt's own right to silence, which I think the Court should put on the balance against the demands of the Government, if any balancing process is to be tolerated.

Moreover, I cannot agree with the Court's notion that First Amendment freedoms must be abridged in order to "preserve" our country. That notion rests on the unarticulated premise that this Nation's security hangs upon its power to punish people because of what they think, speak or write about, or because of those with whom they associate for political purposes. I agree that despotic governments cannot exist without stifling the voice of opposition to their oppressive practices. The First Amendment means to me, however, that the only constitutional way our Government can preserve itself is to leave its people the fullest possible freedom to praise, criticize or discuss, as they see fit, all governmental policies and to suggest, if they desire, that even its most fundamental postulates are bad and should be changed. . . .

The Court implies, however, that the ordinary rules and requirements of the Constitution do not apply because the Committee is merely after Communists and they do not constitute a political party but only a criminal gang. Of course it has always been recognized that members of the Party who, either individually or in combination, commit acts in violation of valid laws can be prosecuted. But the Party as a whole and innocent members of it could not be attainted merely because it had some illegal aims and because some of its members were law-breakers.

Finally, I think Barenblatt's conviction violates the Constitution because the chief aim, purpose and practice of the House Un-American Activities Committee, as disclosed by its many reports, is to try witnesses and punish them because they are or have been Communists or because they refuse to admit or deny Communist affiliations. The punishment imposed is generally punishment by humiliation and public shame.

Ultimately all the questions in this case really boil down to one—whether we as a people will try fearfully and futilely to preserve democracy by adopting totalitarian methods, or whether in accordance with our traditions and our Constitution we will have the confidence and courage to be free.

I would reverse this conviction.

XII

FREEDOM OF SPEECH AND OF THE PRESS: OPINION AND ASSOCIATION

The State of New Mexico refused to admit one Schware to the bar because he had been, as he conceded, a member of the Communist Party. The Supreme Court, in 1957, ordered his admission, holding that one was not precluded from practicing law by reason of holding political or economic views repugnant to the orthodox. [*Schware v. New Mexico*, 353 U.S. 232] But a State may compel an applicant for admission to the bar to answer questions about his beliefs and opinions to determine, for example, whether he believes in the violent overthrow of the government. [*Konigsberg v. State Bar*, 366 U.S. 36 (1961)]

Tax exemption, however, the Court held, could not be denied to a veteran or a church because of the refusal to execute an affidavit that the veteran was not a Communist or that the church was not a Communist front. Ideas are not to be controlled by granting or withholding tax exemption. [*Speiser v. Randall*, 357 U.S. 513 (1958); *First Unitarian Church v. Los Angeles*, 357 U.S. 545 (1958)] This followed earlier cases in which taxes on newspapers [*Grosjean v. American Press Co.*, the Court's opinion, in abridgment, is at page 109.] and on churches [*Follett v. Town of McCormick*, 321 U.S. 573 (1944)] were held unconstitutional as impairing First Amendment rights.

Among the most important of the decisions in this area was the Court's order vacating a judgment of the Alabama courts requiring the National Association for the Advancement of Colored People to deliver to the State its list of members. The NAACP refused to divulge to Alabama the names of its members, arguing that to do so would be an invasion of their individual right of privacy, freedom of opinion, and freedom of association. This argument was sustained by the Court's judgment that the Fourteenth Amendment requirements of due process made this inquiry into the identity of the members of the NAACP a violation of their First Amendment right to freedom of expression. [*National Association for the Advancement of Colored People v. Alabama*, 357 U.S. 449 (1958); also see *Louisiana v. NAACP*, 366 U.S. 293 (1961)]

However, in 1959, the Supreme Court upheld the right of the State of New Hampshire to demand the names of guests at a summer study camp sponsored by an organization called the World Fellowship. The State Attorney General had been commissioned by the Legislature to investigate subversion within the State's borders. The Court found that there was sufficient evidence that the investigation might reveal the identities of subversive persons and that the State's interest in its self-preservation was paramount to the First Amendment rights of the Fellowship's guests to freedom of association and belief. [*Uphaus v. Wyman;* the dissenting opinion, in abridgment, is at page 112.]

In a 1928 case, the Court ruled similarly in upholding a New York statute that required organizations such as the Ku Klux Klan to disclose the names of their members. The Court, because of the history of unlawful intimidation and violence by the Klan, held that New York was warranted in subordinating the First Amendment rights of the Klan and its members. [*Bryant v. Zimmerman*, 278 U.S. 63; also see *Communist Party v. Subversive Activities Control Board*, 367 U.S. 1 (1961)]

The rule is that a determination must be made of the nature and activities of the organization whose membership list is requested, and upon a finding that its members are or may be engaged in antisocial or antidemocratic activities, then the organization is required to disclose names despite the First Amendment rights of its members to freedom of association and to privacy.

This rule seems reasonable enough, but who is to determine what is antisocial or antidemocratic activity? The *World Fellowship* case, as Justice Brennan said in his dissenting opinion, shows that merely holding an unpopular or dissident opinion may under this rule be the excuse for requiring the publication of the names of members of a group. And, said Justice Brennan, this serves no legislative purpose but is "a roving, self-contained investigation of individual and group behavior, and behavior in a constitutionally protected area" for the sole purpose of "[E]xposure purely for the sake of exposure." The Chief Justice and Justices Black and Douglas concurred in the dissent saying the contempt conviction of Uphaus was justifiable only "If bills of attainder were still a legitimate legislative end. . . ."

Arkansas in 1958 enacted a statute (Act 10) that no person might be employed in the public schools or universities unless he annually filed an affidavit naming, without limitation, every organization to which he belonged or to which he regularly contributed in the preceding five years. Many States, in recent years, have adopted similar statutes. Some were concerned with subversive organizations, others were principally aimed at determining which teachers were members of the National Association for the Advancement of Colored People.

Three teachers who had not been reappointed because they refused to sign the Arkansas all-inclusive affidavits brought the question of the validity of their terminations to the Supreme Court. One had refused to file any affidavit, but evidence at the trial showed he had never belonged to a subversive organization. Another of the petitioners had filed an affidavit disclosing membership in the Arkansas Education Association and the American Legion and stating that he had never belonged to a subversive organization. The third petitioner executed an affirmation listing membership in professional organizations and denying having ever been a member of a subversive organization.

The Court said that a State has the right to investigate the competence of its teachers, but that the scope of this inquiry under the Arkansas statute was completely unlimited as it required the listing of churches, political parties, political organizations, and social and professional organizations, many of which have no bearing on a teacher's occupational competence or fitness.

The Supreme Court reversed the Arkansas judgment sustaining the terminations, holding that the statute violated the constitutionally protected right to freedom of opinion and association, saying:

> The statute does not provide that the information it requires be kept confidential. . . . The record contains evidence to indicate that fear of public disclosure is neither theoretical or groundless. . . . [Public exposure of teachers] who belong to unpopular or minority organizations, would simply operate to widen and aggravate the impairment of constitutional liberty. . . . Though the governmental purpose be legitimate and substantial, that purpose cannot be pursued by means that broadly stifle fundamental personal liberties when the end can be more narrowly achieved. [*Shelton v. Tucker*, 364 U.S. 479 (1960)]

Included in the freedom to speak is the right to privacy, or the right not to speak. The Jehovah's Witnesses, who have been parties in Court cases involving this right, are a devout sect, each of whose members is considered a missionary clergyman and is obligated to work for the conversion of the unbelievers. While they are completely intolerant of religious views other than their own, they have served the nation well in fighting case after case in the interest of freedom of speech, assembly, and religion.

Children of Jehovah's Witnesses refused on religious grounds to salute the flag and pledge allegiance as required by law in the West Virginia schools. They objected that the flag was a "graven image" in the sense forbidden by the Bible. The penalty for the children was expulsion from school, and then detention as juvenile delinquents; for the parents the penalty was imprisonment for causing delinquency. The Court invalidated the West Virginia statute as violative of the First and Fourteenth Amendments, saying, "If there is any fixed star in our constitutional constellation, it is that no official, high or petty, can prescribe what shall be orthodox in politics, nationalism, religion, or other matters of opinion or force citizens to confess by word or act their faith therein." [*West Virginia v. Barnette*, 319 U.S. 624 (1943)]

Another right collateral to the right to speak is the right to listen. This question also was brought to the Court by a Jehovah's Witness, one Marsh, who for distributing religious literature on a sidewalk in a "company town" was convicted by an Alabama court on the charge of remaining on private property after being warned to leave. The town, though privately owned and containing no public streets or other facilities, was freely used by the public. But people living in a company town are not deprived of their freedom of speech and equal protection of the laws. In the reversal of the conviction of Marsh, the Jehovah's Witness, the rights sustained for him were only incidental to the more important right of the town's residents to hear what he had to say. Weighing personal rights of freedom against property rights, Justice Black said: "When we balance the Constitutional rights of owners of property against those of the people to enjoy freedom of press and religion, as we must here, we remain mindful of the fact that the latter occupy a preferred position." [*Marsh v. Alabama*, 326 U.S. 501 (1946)]

At the same term, the Court had before it another Jehovah's Witness case identical with *Marsh*, except that the arrest was for trespassing on Hondo Navigation Village, Texas, a private area entirely owned and administered by the Federal Public Housing Authority. The Court held that ownership by the United States did not make the situation other than that in *Marsh*, and the conviction was reversed on the same reasoning as an infringement of the First Amendment freedoms. [*Tucker v. Texas*, 326 U.S. 517 (1946)]

While the Court sustained in these cases the right to listen, it has also asserted for citizens the right of privacy or the right not to listen. For example, a door-to-door solicitor of subscriptions to national magazines unsuccessfully appealed his conviction of violating a municipal ordinance prohibiting peddlers and solicitors going to residences. The rationale of sustaining the prohibitory ordinance was that a community could, if it wished, protect its inhabitants from being disturbed by peddlers even if they were selling magazines, as this protection was not violative of the freedom of the press. [*Breard v. Alexandria*, 341 U.S. 622 (1951)] On the other hand, in an earlier case an ordinance which prohibited the distribution of circulars but did not have any reference to peddling or soliciting was held invalid. The Court, reversing the conviction as an impairment of freedom of religion and the press, said: "The ordinance does not control anything but the distribution of literature, and in that respect it substitutes the judgment of the community for the judgment of the individual householder." [*Martin v. Struthers,* 319 U.S. 141 (1943)]

GROSJEAN v. AMERICAN PRESS CO., 297 U.S. 233 (1935)

Abridgment of Mr. Justice Sutherland's Opinion for the Court.

This suit was brought by . . . nine publishers of newspapers in the State of Louisiana, to enjoin the enforcement against them of the provisions of § 1 of the act of the legislature of Louisiana known as Act No. 23, passed and approved July 12, 1934, as follows:

> "That every person, firm, association, or corporation, . . . engaged in the business of selling, or making any charge for, advertising or for advertisements, whether printed or published, . . . in any newspaper, . . . having a circulation of more than 20,000 copies per week, . . . in the State of Louisiana, shall, . . . pay a license tax for the privilege of engaging in such business in this state of two per cent. (2%) of the gross receipts of such business."

The nine publishers who brought the suit publish thirteen newspapers; and these thirteen publications are the only ones within the State of Louisiana having each a circulation of more than 20,000 copies per week, . . . The revenue derived from appellees' newspapers comes almost entirely from regular subscribers or purchasers thereof and from payments received for the insertion of advertisements therein.

The validity of the act is assailed as violating the Federal Constitution . . . that it abridges the freedom of the press in contravention of the due process clause contained in § 1 of the Fourteenth Amendment. . . .

The tax imposed is designated a "license tax for the privilege of engaging in such business"—that is to say, the business of selling, or making any charge for, advertising. As applied to appellees, it is a tax of two per cent. on the gross receipts derived from advertisements carried in their newspapers when, and only when, the newspapers of each enjoy a circulation of more than 20,000 copies per week. It thus operates as a restraint in a double sense. First, its effect is to curtail the amount of revenue realized from advertising, and, second, its direct tendency is to restrict circulation. This is plain enough when we consider that, if it were increased to a high degree, as it could be if valid, it well might result in destroying both advertising and circulation.

A determination of the question whether the tax is valid in respect of the point now under review, requires an examination of the history and circumstances which antedated and attended the adoption of the abridgment clause of the First Amendment, since that clause expresses one of those "fundamental principles of liberty and justice which lie at the base of all our civil and political institutions" and, as such, is embodied in the concept "due process of law" and, therefore, protected against hostile state invasion by the due process clause of the Fourteenth Amendment. The history is a long one; but for present purposes it may be greatly abbreviated.

For more than a century prior to the adoption of the amendment—and, indeed, for many years thereafter—history discloses a persistent effort on the part of the British government to prevent or abridge the free expression of any opinion which seemed to criticize or exhibit in an unfavorable light, however truly, the agencies and operations of the government. The struggle between the proponents of measures to that end and those who asserted the right of free expression was continuous and unceasing.

In 1712, in response to a message from Queen Anne, Parliament imposed a tax upon all newspapers and upon advertisements. That the main purpose of these taxes was to suppress the publication of comments and criticisms objectionable to the Crown does not admit of doubt. There followed more than a century of resistance to, and evasion of, the taxes, and of agitation for their repeal. [T]hese taxes constituted one of the factors that aroused the American colonists to protest against taxation for the purposes of the home government; and that the revolution really began when, in 1765, that government sent stamps for newspaper duties to the American colonies.

These duties were quite commonly characterized as "taxes on knowledge," a phrase used for the purpose of describing the effect of the exactions and at the same time condemning them. That the taxes had, and were intended to have, the effect of curtailing the circulation of newspapers, and particularly the cheaper ones whose readers were generally found among the masses of the people, went almost without question, even on the part of those who defended the act.

It is idle to suppose that so many of the best men of England would for a century of time have waged, as they did, stubborn and often precarious warfare against these taxes if a mere matter of taxation had been involved. The aim of the struggle was not to relieve taxpayers from a burden, but to establish and preserve the right of the English people to full information in respect of the doings or misdoings of their government.

The framers of the First Amendment were familiar with the English struggle, which then had continued for nearly eighty years and was destined to go on for another sixty-five years, at the end of which time it culminated in a lasting abandonment of the obnoxious taxes. It is impossible to concede that by the words "freedom of the press" the framers of the amendment intended to adopt merely the narrow view then reflected by the law of England that such freedom consisted only in immunity from previous censorship; for this abuse had then permanently disappeared from English practice. It is equally impossible to believe that it was not intended to bring within the reach of these words such modes of restraint as were embodied in the two forms of taxation already described.

In the light of all that has now been said, it is evident that the restricted rules of the English law in respect of the freedom of the press in force when the Constitution was adopted were never accepted by the American colonists, and that by the First Amendment it was meant to preclude the national government, and by the Fourteenth Amendment to preclude the states, from adopting any form of previous restraint upon printed publications, or their circulation, including that which had theretofore been effected by these two well-known and odious methods.

The tax here involved is bad not because it takes money from the pockets of the appellees. If that were all, a wholly different question would be presented. It is bad because, in the light of its history and of its present setting, it is seen to be a deliberate and calculated device in the guise of a tax to limit the circulation of information to which the public is entitled in virtue of the constitutional guaranties. A free press stands as one of the great interpreters between the government and the people. To allow it to be fettered is to fetter ourselves.

Decree affirmed.

UPHAUS v. WYMAN, 360 U.S. 72 (1959)

Abridgment of Dissenting Opinion of Mr. Justice Brennan, with whom Mr. Chief Justice Warren, Mr. Justice Black, and Mr. Justice Douglas concurred.

The Court holds today that the constitutionally protected rights of speech and assembly of appellant and those whom he may represent are to be subordinated to New Hampshire's legislative investigation because, as applied in the demands made on him, the investigation is rationally connected with a discernible legislative purpose. With due respect for my Brothers' views, I do not agree that a showing of any requisite legislative purpose or other state interest that constitutionally can subordinate appellant's rights is to be found in this record. Exposure purely for the sake of exposure is not such a valid subordinating purpose.

It was logical that the adverse effects of unwanted publicity—of exposure—as concomitants of the exercise of the investigatory power, should come to be recognized, in certain circumstances, as invading protected freedoms and offending constitutional inhibitions upon governmental actions. For in an era of mass communications and mass opinion, and of international tensions and domestic anxiety, exposure and group identification by the state of those holding unpopular and dissident views are fraught with such serious consequences for the individual as inevitably to inhibit seriously the expression of views which the Constitution intended to make free.

Government must have freedom to make an appropriate investigation where there appears a rational connection with the law making process, the processes of adjudication, or other essential governmental functions. The problem is one in its nature calling for traditional case-by-case development of principles in the various permutations of circumstances where the conflict may appear. But guide lines must be marked out by the courts. On the facts of this case I think that New Hampshire's investigation, as applied to the appellant, was demonstrably and clearly outside the wide limits of the power which must be conceded to the State even though it be attended by some exposure.

The appellant, Uphaus, is Executive Director of a group called World Fellowship which runs a discussion program at a summer camp in New Hampshire, at which the public is invited to stay. Various speakers come to the camp primarily for discussion of political, economic and social matters. The activities going on were those of private citizens. The views expounded obviously were minority views. But the assemblage, was, on its face, for purposes to which the First and Fourteenth Amendments give constitutional protection against incursion by the powers of government.

The investigation with which this case is concerned was undertaken under authority of a 1953 Resolution of the New Hampshire General Court, . . . The Resolution directed the Attorney General of the State . . . to make a "full and complete investigation" of "violations of the subversive activities act of 1951" and to determine whether "subversive persons as defined in said act are presently located within the state." Under New Hampshire law, this constituted the Attorney General (who is ordinarily the chief law-enforcement official of the State) a one-man legislative committee. [T]he Attorney General was authorized in sweeping terms to give publicity to the details of his investigation.

The fruits of the first two years of the investigation were delivered to the Legislature in a comprehensive volume on January 5, 1955. . . . [T]he report is an official indication of the nature of the investigation and is, in fact, the stated objective of the duty assigned by the Resolution to the Attorney General.

Virtually the entire "Letter of Transmittal" of the Attorney General addressed itself to discussing the policy used in the report in disclosing the names of individuals. The report was not to be considered an indictment of any individual, the Attorney General suitably pointing out that a grand jury was the only authority in New Hampshire having the formal power of indictment. [T]he Attorney General stressed that "[T]he reporting of facts herein does NOT (nor should it be taken to by any reader) constitute a charge against any witness." He observed that "facts are facts. . . . Conclusions of opprobrium relative to any individual, while within the privilege of personal opinion, are neither recommended nor intended to be encouraged by any phraseology of this report." In fact, the listing of names might well contain the names of many innocent people, implied the Attorney General.

The emphasis of the entire report is on individual guilt, individual near-guilt, and individual questionable behavior. Of course, if the Attorney General had information relating to guilt under the statute, he was empowered to seek indictment and conviction of the offenders in criminal proceedings, in which of course the normal rights afforded criminal defendants and the normal limitations on state prosecution for conduct related to political association and expression, under the Constitution, would apply. The citation of names in the book does not appear to have any relation to the possibility of an orthodox or traditional criminal prosecution, and the Attorney General seems to acknowledge this.

The Legislature, upon receiving the report, extended the investigation for a further two years. It was during this period that the refusals of the appellant to furnish information with which we are now concerned took place. The Attorney General had already published the names of speakers at the World Fellowship camp. Now he wanted the correspondence between Uphaus and the speakers. The guest list, the nonavailability of which to the Attorney General was commented on in . . . the 1955 report . . . was also desired. [A]ppellant's failure to respond . . . was found contemptuous.

Most legislative investigations unavoidably involve exposure of some sort or another. But it is quite clear that exposure was the very core, and deliberately and purposefully so, of the legislative investigation we are concerned with here.

One may accept the Court's truism [in the majority opinion] that preservation of the State's existence is undoubtedly a proper purpose for legislation. But, in descending from this peak of abstraction to the facts of this case, one must ask the question: What relation did this investigation of individual conduct have to legislative ends here? If bills of attainder were still a legitimate legislative end, it is clear that the investigations and reports might naturally have furnished the starting point (though only that) for a legislative adjudication of guilt under the 1951 Act. But what other legislative purpose was actually being fulfilled by the course taken by this investigation, with its overwhelming emphasis on individual associations and conduct?

The bare fact that the Legislature has authorized the inquiry does not mean that the inquiry is for a valid legislative end when viewed in the light of the federal constitutional test we must apply.

It is not enough to say, as the Court's position I fear may amount to, that what was taking place was an investigation and until the Attorney General and the Legislature had in all the data, the precise shape of the legislative action to be taken was necessarily unknown. Investigation and exposure, in the area which we are here concerned with, are not recognized as self-contained legislative powers in themselves. Since this is so, it hardly fulfills the responsibility with which this Court is charged, of protecting the constitutional rights of freedom of speech and assembly, to admit that an investigation going on indefinitely in time, roving in subject matter, and cumulative in detail in this area can be in aid of a valid legislative end, on the theory that some day it may come to some point. Even the most abusive investigation, the one most totally committed to the constitutionally impermissible end of individual adjudication through publication, could pass such a test. Nor can we accept the legislative renewal of the investigation, or the taking of other legislative measures to facilitate the investigation, as being themselves the legislative justification of the inquiry. Nor can the faint possibility that an already questionably broad criminal statute might be further broadened, if constitutionally permissible, be considered the subordinating legislative purpose here, . . .

[I]f the principles this Court has announced, and to which the Court today makes some deference, are to have any meaning, it must be up to the State to make some at least plausible disclosure of its law making interest so that the relevance of its inquiries to it may be tested.

[W]e must demand some initial showing by the State sufficient to counterbalance the interest in privacy as it relates to freedom of speech and assembly. On any basis that has practical meaning, New Hampshire has not made such a showing here. I would reverse the judgment of the New Hampshire Supreme Court

XIII

FREEDOM OF SPEECH AND OF THE PRESS: THE RIGHT OF ASSEMBLY

From time to time various municipalities have required licenses before one could hold a public meeting in the parks and streets. Some of these ordinances were simply procedures to place meetings where they would not interfere with traffic. Others, however, were used as a means of censorship. [*De Jonge v. Oregon,* for example; the Court's opinion, in abridgment, is at page 118.]

Again, we meet the ubiquitous Jehovah's Witnesses. Having been refused licenses for several successive Sundays, they held a meeting in a public park in Havre de Grace, Maryland, without a permit. The Court invalidated the ordinance requiring licenses as censorship by prior restraint in contravention of the Fourteenth Amendment requirement that no State "shall abridge the privileges" of citizens. The Court also found a violation of the same Amendment's guarantee of "equal protection of the laws" in that licenses had been issued for other meetings to persons who wished to advance more popular views. [*Niemotko v. Maryland,* 340 U.S. 268 (1951)]

At the same term during which the Maryland Jehovah's Witness case was decided, the Court held unconstitutional, as a prior restraint on freedom of speech, a New York City ordinance requiring permits for public street meetings. Kunz, an itinerant preacher, was refused a permit because he engaged in hate-stirring attacks on Catholics and Jews. Though the Court reversed his conviction, Justice Jackson dissented, saying that while New York City would be prohibited as a prior restraint from preventing Kunz's speaking in a pulpit or hall, it was not required to "place its streets at his service to hurl insults at the passerby." [*Kunz v. New York,* 340 U.S. 290 (1951)]

Also from New York, though from the upstate city of Syracuse, came an appeal to the Court from a university student named Feiner who, at a street meeting addressing seventy-five or eighty persons, denounced and vilified President Truman, the Mayor of Syracuse, and the American Legion. His conviction was for disorderly conduct in refusing to stop speaking on the request of the police when they thought rioting might ensue. The Court held that his arrest was proper as freedom of speech does not include the right to disturb the peace. But Justice Black, in a dissent in which he was joined by two other Justices, argued forcefully that First and Fourteenth Amendment rights might become meaningless if the police may arbitrarily determine that any unrest or dissent in an audience justifies a conclusion that the speaker is inducing a breach of the peace. The duty of the police is to quiet or arrest the heckler and not the speaker. [*Feiner v. New York,* 340 U.S. 315 (1951)]

DE JONGE v. OREGON,
299 U.S. 353 (1937)

Abridgment of Mr. Chief Justice Hughes' Opinion for the Court.

Dirk De Jonge was indicted in Multnomah County, Oregon, for violation of the Criminal Syndicalism Law of that State. It . . . appears that, while defendant was a member of the Communist Party, he was not indicted for participating in its organization, or for joining it, or for soliciting members or for distributing its literature. He was not charged with teaching or advocating criminal syndicalism or sabotage or any unlawful acts, either at the meeting or elsewhere. His sole offense as charged, and for which he was convicted and sentenced to imprisonment for seven years, was that he had assisted in the conduct of a public meeting, albeit otherwise lawful, which was held under the auspices of the Communist Party.

The broad reach of the statute as thus applied is plain. While defendant was a member of the Communist Party, that membership was not necessary to conviction on such a charge. A like fate might have attended any speaker, although not a member, who "assisted in the conduct" of the meeting. However innocuous the object of the meeting, however lawful the subjects and tenor of the addresses, however reasonable and timely the discussion, all those assisting in the conduct of the meeting would be subject to imprisonment as felons if the meeting were held by the Communist Party.

While the States are entitled to protect themselves from the abuse of the privileges of our institutions through an attempted substitution of force and violence in the place of peaceful political action in order to effect revolutionary changes in government, none of our decisions go to the length of sustaining such a curtailment of the right of free speech and assembly as the Oregon statute demands in its present application.

Freedom of speech and of the press are fundamental rights which are safeguarded by the due process clause of the Fourteenth Amendment of the Federal Constitution.

These rights may be abused by using speech or press or assembly in order to incite to violence and crime. The people through their legislatures may protect themselves against that abuse. But the legislative intervention can find constitutional justification only by dealing with the abuse. The rights themselves must not be curtailed. The greater the importance of safeguarding the community from incitements to the overthrow of our institutions by force and violence, the more imperative is the need to preserve inviolate the constitutional rights of free speech, free press and free assembly in order to maintain the opportunity for free political discussion, to the end that government may be responsive to the will of the people and that changes, if desired, may be obtained by peaceful means. Therein lies the security of the Republic, the very foundation of constitutional government.

It follows from these considerations that, consistently with the Federal Constitution, peaceable assembly for lawful discussion cannot be made a crime. The question, if the rights of free speech and peaceable assembly are to be preserved, is not as to the auspices under which the meeting is held but as to its purpose; not as to the relations of the speakers, but whether their utterances transcend the bounds of the freedom of speech which the Constitution protects.

We hold that the Oregon statute as applied to the particular charge as defined by the state court is repugnant to the due process clause of the Fourteenth Amendment. The judgment of conviction is reversed and the cause is remanded for further proceedings not inconsistent with this opinion.

XIV

FREEDOM OF SPEECH AND OF THE PRESS: PASSPORTS

In 1958 the Court struck down the power assumed by the State Department to deny passports, without confrontation by witnesses and specifications of charges, to those it suspected had at some time been members of the Communist Party or of organizations it considered Communist fronts. The holding of unorthodox or unpopular opinions, or association with others holding such opinions, are not grounds on which the Department of State may deny a citizen the right to travel. Since this *Rockwell Kent* decision, the State Department issues passports generally and asserts the right of refusal only when it claims the passport will help in the commission of overt acts of disloyalty to the United States. Questions about what one thought or whether one was or had ever been a member of the Communist Party or of an organization advocating the violent overthrow of the government, were held improper questions for the State Department to address to a passport applicant.

The only other restrictions on passports are geographical or area limitations on the use of a passport which apply to all Americans.

Immediately after the *Rockwell Kent* decision, the President asked Congress for legislation to overcome the effect of the Court's ruling. Several bills were introduced in the Eighty-sixth Congress which would have given the State Department the right to deny passports because of the beliefs or associations of the applicant. These bills did not require the specification of charges and the quasi-judicial hearing that the Court said was required before a passport application could be denied. Nor did the bills differentiate between belief and action, or even the reasonable likelihood of action, prejudicial to the interests of the United States. But such was the educative value of the Court's action that Congress did not pass any of these measures. It heeded the Court's ruling that "the right to travel is a part of the 'liberty' of which the citizen cannot be deprived without due process of law of the Fifth Amendment." [*Kent v. Dulles*; the Court's opinion, in abridgment, follows immediately; but see page 122 for a discussion of *Communist Party v. Subversive Activities Control Board.*]

KENT v. DULLES, 357 U.S. 116 (1958)

Abridgment of Mr. Justice Douglas' Opinion for the Court. (Mr. Justice Clark dissented in an opinion in which Mr. Justice Harlan, Mr. Justice Burton, and Mr. Justice Whittaker concurred.)

This case concerns two applications for passports, denied by the Secretary of State. One was by Rockwell Kent who desired to visit England and attend a meeting of an organization known as the "World Council of Peace" in Helsinki, Finland. The Director of the Passport Office informed Kent that issuance of a passport was precluded by . . . the Regulations promulgated by the Secretary of State on two grounds: (1) that he was a Communist and (2) that he had had "a consistent and prolonged adherence to the Communist Party line."

Kent sued in the District Court for declaratory relief. The District Court granted summary judgment for respondent. On appeal the case of Kent was heard with that of Dr. Walter Briehl, a psychiatrist. When Briehl applied for a passport, the Director of the Passport Office asked him to supply the affidavit covering membership in the Communist Party. Briehl, like Kent, refused.

The right to travel is a part of the "liberty" of which the citizen cannot be deprived without due process of law under the Fifth Amendment. So much is conceded by the Solicitor General. In Anglo-Saxon law that right was emerging at least as early as the Magna Carta. Travel abroad, like travel within the country, may be necessary for a livelihood. It may be as close to the heart of the individual as the choice of what he eats, or wears, or reads. Freedom of movement is basic in our scheme of values.

Since we start with an exercise by an American citizen of an activity included in constitutional protection, we will not readily infer that Congress gave the Secretary of State unbridled discretion to grant or withhold it. If we were dealing with political questions entrusted to the Chief Executive by the Constitution we would have a different case. But there is more involved here. In part, of course, the issuance of the passport carries some implication of intention to extend the bearer diplomatic protection, though it does no more than "request all whom it may concern to permit safely and freely to pass, and in case of need to give all lawful aid and protection" to this citizen of the United States. But that function of the passport is subordinate. Its crucial function today is control over exit. And, as we have seen, the right of exit is a personal right included within the word "liberty" as used in the Fifth Amendment. If that "liberty" is to be regulated, it must be pursuant to the law-making functions of the Congress. Where activities or enjoyment, natural and often necessary to the well-being of an American citizen, such as travel, are involved, we will construe narrowly all delegated powers that curtail or dilute them. We hesitate to find in this broad generalized power an authority to trench so heavily on the rights of the citizen.

Thus we do not reach the question of constitutionality. We only conclude that [Congress did] not delegate to the Secretary the kind of authority exercised here. We deal with beliefs, with associations, with ideological matters. We must remember that we are dealing here with citizens who have neither been accused of crimes nor found guilty. They are being denied their freedom of movement solely because of their refusal to be subjected to inquiry into their beliefs and associations. They do not seek to escape the law nor to violate it.

We would be faced with important constitutional questions were we to hold that Congress . . . had given the Secretary authority to withhold passports to citizens because of their beliefs or associations. Congress has made no such provision in explicit terms; and absent one, the Secretary may not employ that standard to restrict the citizens' right of free movement.

Reversed.

XV

FREEDOM OF SPEECH AND OF THE PRESS: GROUP LIBEL

Language in defamation of another person is slanderous if spoken and libelous if written. Such words are not protected by the Constitution and are actionable at law. But if the defamatory utterance concerns a public official or a candidate for public office then the importance to society of protecting the right to talk is greater than the importance of protecting the reputation of the individual. But neither the laws of the several States nor the court decisions are in agreement as to this differentiation, and there has been no determination by the United States Supreme Court.

Whether libel of racial and religious groups is actionable has engaged scholars in controversy, particularly since Hitler came upon the world scene and his counterparts in the United States have variously and scurrilously attacked Negroes, Catholics and Jews. Most liberals have taken the position that to prohibit such expression would be dangerous interference with freedom of speech that would necessarily lead to other inhibitions. There is force in their argument that it is but one step from prohibiting libel of a religious or racial group to forbidding libel of a political party—a possibility which raises specters from the days of seditious libel. A minority of legal writers and only a few States make group libel a crime or grant a cause of action for damages to an individual who is a member of a libeled class.

Attempts to pass a group libel law in Congress have failed, but the Court upheld the constitutionality of an Illinois group libel statute when it was challenged by one Beauharnais, a professional white supremacy advocate. He solicited membership in the White Circle League of America, Inc., with a leaflet portraying all Negroes as depraved, criminal, and unchaste. He called on the Mayor and City Council of Chicago to stop the "invasion of white people, their property, neighborhoods and persons, by the negro" and asked white people to resist being "mongrelized by the negro" and said they were in danger of "rapes, robberies, knives, guns and marijuana of the negro." The Court affirmed the conviction of Beauharnais in the State courts, saying that Illinois had not deprived him of his right to freedom of speech and that the Illinois penal statute was constitutional. [*Beauharnais v. Illinois;* an abridgment of the Court's opinion is at page 127 and of a dissenting opinion at page 126. For a discussion of "Pure Races," and "The Assumption that Cultural Level is Dependent upon Racial Attributes," see Weinberger, "A Reappraisal of the Constitutionality of Miscegenation Statutes," *Cornell Law Quarterly,* Winter, 1957 (revised to date, but without footnotes, *Journal of the National Medical Association,* May, 1959).]

The fears of the liberals who oppose group libel laws are farfetched. They are putting theoretical fears above the practicalities of life. True, one should defend the right to speak even if it is the right of those with whom one disagrees. But if there is no danger to democracy in reasonable criminal laws directed to libel of an individual, then similarly there is none in making criminal the libel of a race or religion. In any event, the danger that such a prohibition would be unduly extended to civil actions for damages or otherwise is less than the harm done by the professional and opportunist hatemongers.

BEAUHARNAIS v. ILLINOIS
343 U.S. 250 (1952)

Abridgment of Mr. Justice Frankfurter's Opinion for the Court.

No one will gainsay that it is libelous falsely to charge another with being a rapist, robber, carrier of knives and guns, and user of marijuana. The precise question before us, then, is whether the protection of "liberty" in the Due Process Clause of the Fourteenth Amendment prevents a State from punishing such libels—as criminal libel has been defined, limited and constitutionally recognized time out of mind—directed at designated collectivities and flagrantly disseminated.

Illinois did not have to look beyond her own borders or await the tragic experience of the last three decades to conclude that wilful purveyors of falsehood concerning racial and religious groups promote strife and tend powerfully to obstruct the manifold adjustments required for free, ordered life in a metropolitan, polyglot community. From the murder of the abolitionist Lovejoy in 1837 to the Cicero riots of 1951, Illinois has been the scene of exacerbated tension between races, often flaring into violence and destruction. In many of these outbreaks, utterances of the character here in question, so the Illinois legislature could conclude, played a significant part.

In the face of this history and its frequent obligato of extreme racial and religious propaganda, we would deny experience to say that the Illinois legislature was without reason in seeking ways to curb false or malicious defamation of racial and religious groups, made in public places and by means calculated to have a powerful emotional impact on those to whom it was presented.

That the legislative remedy might not in practice mitigate the evil, or might itself raise new problems, would only manifest once more the paradox of reform. It is the price to be paid for the trial-and-error inherent in legislative efforts to deal with obstinate social issues. Certainly the Due Process Clause does not require the legislature to be in the vanguard of science—especially sciences as young as human ecology and cultural anthropology.

Long ago this Court recognized that the economic rights of an individual may depend for the effectiveness of their enforcement on rights in the group, even though not formally corporate, to which he belongs. Such group-protection on behalf of the individual may, for all we know, be a need not confined to the part that a trade union plays in effectuating rights abstractly recognized as belonging to its members. It is not within our competence to confirm or deny claims of social scientists as to the dependence of the individual on the position of his racial or religious group in the community. This being so, we are precluded from saying that speech concededly punishable when immediately directed at individuals cannot be outlawed if directed at groups with whose position and esteem in society the affiliated individual may be inextricably involved.

Affirmed

Abridgment of Dissenting Opinion of Mr. Justice Black. (Mr. Justice Reed, Mr. Justice Douglas, and Mr. Justice Jackson also dissented in separate opinions.)

[T]he Illinois statute emerges labeled a "group libel law." This label may make the Court's holding more palatable for those who sustain it, but the sugar-coating does not make the censorship less deadly. However tagged, the Illinois law is not that criminal libel which has been "defined, limited and constitutionally recognized time out of mind." For as "constitutionally recognized" that crime has provided for punishment of false, malicious, scurrilous charges against individuals, not against huge groups. This limited scope of the law of criminal libel is of no small importance. It has confined state punishment of speech and expression to the narrowest of areas involving nothing more than purely private feuds. Every expansion of the law of criminal libel so as to punish discussions of matters of public concern means a corresponding invasion of the area dedicated to free expression by the First Amendment.

In other words, in arguing for or against the enactment of laws that may differently affect huge groups, it is now very dangerous indeed to say something critical of one of the groups. And any "person, firm or corporation" can be tried for this crime. "Person, firm or corporation" certainly includes a book publisher, newspaper, radio or television station, candidate or even a preacher.

It is easy enough to say that none of this latter group have been proceeded against under the Illinois Act. And they have not—yet. But emotions bubble and tempers flare in racial and religious controversies, the kind here involved.

This Act sets up a system of state censorship which is at war with the kind of free government envisioned by those who forced adoption

of our Bill of Rights. The motives behind the state law may have
been to do good. But the same can be said about most laws making
opinions punishable as crimes. History indicates that urges to do
good have led to the burning of books and even to the burning of
"witches."

No rationalization on a purely legal level can conceal the fact that
state laws like this one present a constant overhanging threat to
freedom of speech, press and religion. Today Beauharnais is punished
for publicly expressing strong views in favor of segregation. Ironically
enough, Beauharnais, convicted of crime in Chicago, would probably
be given a hero's reception in many other localities, if not in some
parts of Chicago itself. Moreover, the same kind of state law that
makes Beauharnais a criminal for advocating segregation in Illinois
can be utilized to send people to jail in other states for for advocating
equality and nonsegregation. What Beauharnais said in his leaflet is
mild compared with usual arguments on both sides of racial controversies.

We are told that freedom of petition and discussion are in no
danger "while this Court sits." This case raises considerable doubt.

If there be minority groups who hail this holding as their victory,
they might consider the possible relevancy of this ancient remark:

"Another such victory and I am undone."

XVI

FREEDOM OF SPEECH AND OF THE PRESS: CENSORSHIP

Despite the freedom of the press guaranteed by the First Amendment, both the Federal government and the various States may suppress obscene publications. The Federal government takes jurisdiction through its control of the mail and the customs; the States, through their power to regulate and control the moral and physical well-being of their citizens. This duality has resulted at times in the same book being freely sold in some States and suppressed in others, and in a publication being passed by the customs and then treated as obscene either by the Post Office or by one of the States.

The courts have been vexed by the lack of definition of obscenity. The statutes indiscriminately use such words as lewd, lascivious, salacious, indecent, filthy and disgusting, or define obscenity as that which tends to stir sexual impulses or leads to sexually impure thoughts. With this vast catalog of words, there is no uniformly accepted definition of what is obscene, although the authorities agree that obscenity encompasses only publications dealing with sex, though at least one State includes excretion in prurient interests. There is agreement that the publication as a whole and not isolated words or passages must be considered, and that the classics are exempt. Aside from these areas of agreement, the standards have varied from time to time and from State to State, creating the anomaly that literature banned in one place may be purchased freely in another.

In England, the test of obscenity enunciated in the middle of the nineteenth century continues to be the law. There, obscene matter is defined as that which tends to corrupt or deprave those whose minds are open to such immoral influences and into whose hands a publication of this sort may fall. [*Regina v. Hicklin*, L.R. 3 Q.B. 360 (1868)] This was also the law in the United States until recently, but it was found unsatisfactory as enforcement of this test would reduce the literature available to the general public to the kinds acceptable for children, the mentally unfit, and the morally perverted. There developed, therefore, what has been called the modern rule, which is that the publication is tested against the effect it will have on the average man. As Judge Woolsey, in the famous *Ulysses* case, put it: ". . . a . . . book . . . must be tested . . . as to its effect on a person with average sex instincts—what the French would call *l'homme moyen sensual.*" [*United States v. One Book Called "Ulysses"*, 5 F. Supp. 182 (1933); affd. 72 F. 2d. 705 (1934)]

Many scholars in the field, and some judges, too, are dissatisfied with this "average or ordinary man" rule. Their position is that all publications, other than outright pornography or "dirt for dirt's sake," are within the First Amendment protection of communication, and that works dealing with sexual behavior should not be equated with the standards and values of the average man. Certainly, religion, economics, politics, philosophy or the classics are not required to conform to what is usual or "average or ordinary."

In 1957 the Supreme Court for the first time defined obscenity. The majority of the Court found the "average or ordinary man" rule to be the law. It held that the proper test was whether or not the publication would arouse improper sexual thoughts in the average person in the community, and that this was a determination to be made by the judge or jury trying the facts. [*Roth v. United States*; the Court's opinion, in abridgment, is at page 135.]

While in theory we now have a national rule, nevertheless, empirically, the standards will differ from jurisdiction to jurisdiction, for the mores of each community will enter into the decisions of the judges and the verdicts of the juries who determine what is obscene to the average man.

When printing was introduced it was assumed, in England as elsewhere, to be under the control and coercion of the government. Presses required licenses, and publications were submitted for prior approval. This censorship was first enforced by the King's proclamations, prohibitions, and licenses and later was administered by the Star Chamber. After the Star Chamber's abolition in 1641, the licensing continued under the control of Parliament even during the Commonwealth. The last of the licensing statutes expired in England in 1695 and in the colonies in 1725.

The principal reason for the prior restraint or censorship of the press was to prevent criticism of the King, of any public man, of the law, or of any institution established by law. All criticism was considered seditious libel. That the criticism was true was no defense. The doctrine of seditious libel and the justification of prior restraint were based on the political concept that the people were the servants of the rulers as opposed to the view, which gained strength in the seventeenth and eighteenth centuries, that the rulers were the agents and servants of the people.

There were many seditious libel prosecutions in England and several in the colonies, including the Peter Zenger trial, in the half-century before the adoption of the Constitution. The Sedition Act of 1798, during its two year life, suppressed the free press in the new republic. The history of seditious libel in England and in the colonies was the motivating force behind the adoption of the First Amendment.

A Minnesota statute of 1925 provided that if a newspaper or periodical was (1) obscene, lewd, and lascivious or (2) malicious, scandalous, and defamatory, an injunction could be issued suppressing the newspaper or periodical and prohibiting further publication. *The Saturday Press* published a series of articles charging that gambling, bootlegging, and racketeering were rife in Minneapolis and that the Chief of Police and other city officials were grossly neglecting their duties, had illicit relationships with gangsters, and participated in graft. In a court action brought by the City Prosecutor, the newspaper did not satisfy the trial judge that the charges were true and published with good motives and for justifiable ends. An injunction was issued against further publication of *The Saturday Press* in the manner of the censor who—it had been thought—had left the American scene a century and a half earlier.

The Supreme Court invalidated the statute as an infringement of the freedom of the press guaranteed by the Fourteenth Amendment, saying:

> . . . liberty of the press, historically considered and taken up by the Federal Constitution, has meant, principally although not exclusively, immunity from previous restraints or censorship. [*Near v. Minnesota*, 283 U.S. 697 (1931)]

Motion pictures have received special treatment in determining the ambit of the First Amendment protection of free speech and a free press. From the early days of motion pictures there have been exhibition licensing laws in a number of the States. This licensing is prior restraint such as is inconceivable in reference to the press—be it a newspaper or a magazine of fiction or amusement. Motion pictures in 1915 were held to be "a business pure and simple" and "not to be regarded . . . as part of the press of the country or as organs of public opinion." [*Mutual Film Corp. v. Industrial Commission*, 236 U.S. 230] This holding left the States and municipalities free to censor and license motion pictures. Today four of the States—Kansas, Maryland, New York and Virginia—censor motion pictures. There are also motion picture censorship systems in a number of cities: Atlanta, Chicago, Detroit, Fort Worth, Kansas City (Mo.), Pasadena, Portland, Providence, Sacramento, San Angelo (Texas), and Wichita Falls (Texas).

While in 1915 motion pictures may have been little more than spectacles and exhibitions, they have become a means of communication just as a printed work of fiction is a medium of ideas as well as one of entertainment. The Court in 1952, overruled the doctrine of the *Mutual Film Case* and held that:

> . . . motion pictures [are] included within the free speech and free press guaranty of the First and Fourteenth Amendments.

This opinion was given in the *Miracle Case*, in which the Court reversed the banning of the film by the New York licensing authorities. But the holding was not that censorship or licensing of motion pictures was prohibited but only "that under the First and Fourteenth Amendments a state may not ban a film on the basis of a censor's conclusion that it is 'sacrilegious'." [*Burstyn v. Wilson*, 343 U.S. 495 (1952)]

Following the *Miracle Case* there were a number of attacks on particular censorship statutes as so indefinite that licensing was entirely by the whim and prejudice of the censor. The Court found the following standards "not clearly drawn," "vague," or "uncertain," and overruled the censor's denial of permits: "prejudicial to the best interests of the people of said City" [*Gelling v. Texas*, 343 U.S. 960 (1952)]; "immoral," [*Commercial Pictures v. Regents*, 346 U.S. 587 (1954)]; "harmful" [*Superior Films v. Department of Education*, 346 U.S. 587 (1954)]; and "sexual immorality" [*Kingsley International Pictures v. Regents*, 360 U.S. 684 (1959)].

In 1961 the Court was presented for the first time with an attack on film censorship *per se*. The issue of the constitutionality of all motion picture censoring was squarely presented. The city of Chicago requires that a film be approved and licensed before its exhibition. The procedure was described as follows:

> Although the Chicago ordinance designates the Commissioner of Police as the censor, counsel for the city explained that the task is delegated to a group of people, often women. The procedure before Chicago's censor board was found to be as follows according to the testimony of the 'commanding officer of the censor unit' [a police sergeant]:
>
> 'Q. Am I to understand that the procedure is that only these six people are in the room, and perhaps you, at the time the film is shown?
>
> 'A. Yes.
>
> 'Q. Does the distributor ever get a chance to present his views on the picture?
>
> 'A. No, sir.
>
> 'Q. Are other people's views invited, such as drama critics or movie reviewers or writers or artists of some kind; or are they ever asked to comment on the film before the censor board makes its decision?
>
> 'A. No, sir.
>
> 'Q. In other words, it is these six people plus yourself in a relationship that we have not as yet defined who decide whether the picture conforms to the standards set up in the ordinance?
>
> 'A. Yes, sir.' [Footnote 8, Dissenting Opinion of the Chief Justice, *Times Film v. Chicago*, 365 U.S. 43 (1961)]

The exhibitor refused to submit the film to the Police Department censor and was refused a license. The Court upheld the Chicago ordinance, saying:

> The challenge here is to the censor's basic authority; it does not go to any statutory standards employed by the censor. . . . It has never been held that liberty of speech is absolute. Nor has it been suggested that all previous restraints on speech are invalid . . . in *Joseph Burstyn, Inc., v Wilson*, . . . we found motion pictures to be within the guarantees of the First and Fourteenth Amendments, but we added that this was 'not the end of our problem.' . . . At this time we say no more than this—that we are dealing only with motion pictures. [*Times Film v. Chicago;* a dissenting opinion, in abridgment, is at page 138.]

ROTH v. UNITED STATES, ALBERTS v. CALIFORNIA, 354 U.S. 476 (1957)

Abridgment of Mr. Justice Brennan's Opinion for the Court. (Mr. Chief Justice Warren concurred in Alberts and dissented in Roth in a separate opinion. Mr. Justice Douglas dissented in an opinion in which Mr. Justice Black concurred.)

The constitutionality of a criminal obscenity statute is the question in each of these cases. In *Roth,* the primary constitutional question is whether the federal obscenity statute violates the provision of the First Amendment that "Congress shall make no law . . . abridging the freedom of speech, or of the press. . . ." In *Alberts,* the primary constitutional question is whether the obscenity provisions of the California Penal Code invade the freedoms of speech and press as they may be incorporated in the liberty protected from state action by the Due Process Clause of the Fourteenth Amendment.

Roth conducted a business in New York in the publication and sale of books, photographs and magazines. He used circulars and advertising matter to solicit sales. He was convicted by a jury [for] violation of the federal obscenity statute.

Alberts conducted a mail-order business from Los Angeles. He was convicted [for] lewdly keeping for sale obscene and indecent books, and with writing, composing and publishing an obscene advertisement of them, in violation of the California Penal Code.

The dispositive question is whether obscenity is utterance within the area of protected speech and press. Although this is the first time the question has been squarely presented to this Court, either under the First Amendment or under the Fourteenth Amendment, expressions found in numerous opinions indicate that this Court has always assumed that obscenity is not protected by the freedoms of speech and press.

The guaranties of freedom of expression in effect in 10 of the 14 States which by 1792 had ratified the Constitution, gave no absolute protection for every utterance. Thirteen of the 14 States provided for the prosecution of libel, and all of those States made either blasphemy or profanity, or both, statutory crimes. As early as 1712, Massachusetts made it criminal to publish "any filthy, obscene, or profane song, pamphlet, libel or mock sermon" in imitation or mimicking of religious services. Thus, profanity and obscenity were related offenses.

All ideas having even the slightest redeeming social importance—
unorthodox ideas, controversial ideas, even ideas hateful to the
prevailing climate of opinion—have the full protection of the guaranties, unless excludable because they encroach upon the limited area
of more important interests. But implicit in the history of the First
Amendment is the rejection of obscenity as utterly without redeeming social importance.

It is strenuously urged that these obscenity statutes offend the
constitutional guaranties because they punish incitation to impure
sexual *thoughts,* not shown to be related to any overt antisocial
conduct which is or may be incited in the persons stimulated to
such *thoughts.* In *Roth,* the trial judge instructed the jury: "The
words 'obscene, lewd and lascivious' as used in the law, signify that
form of immorality which has relation to sexual impurity and has
a tendency to excite lustful *thoughts.*" (Emphasis added.) In *Alberts,*
the trial judge applied the test . . . whether the material has "a substantial tendency to deprave or corrupt its readers by inciting lascivious *thoughts* or arousing lustful desires." (Emphasis added.) It is
insisted that the constitutional guaranties are violated because convictions may be had without proof either that obscene material will
perceptibly create a clear and present danger of antisocial conduct,
or will probably induce its recipients to such conduct. But, in light
of our holding that obscenity is not protected speech, the complete
answer to this argument is in the holding of this Court in *Beauharnais* v. *Illinois.*

"Libelous utterances not being within the area of constitutionally
protected speech, it is unnecessary, either for us or for the State
courts, to consider the issues behind the phrase 'clear and present
danger.' Certainly no one would contend that obscene speech, for
example, may be punished only upon a showing of such circumstances. . . ."

. . . [s]ex and obscenity are not synonymous. Obscene material is
material which deals with sex in a manner appealing to prurient
interest. The portrayal of sex, e.g., in art, literature and scientific
works, is not itself sufficient reason to deny material the constitutional
protection of freedom of speech and press.

The fundamental freedoms of speech and press have contributed
greatly to the development and well-being of our free society and are
indispensable to its continued growth. Ceaseless vigilance is the

watchword to prevent their erosion by Congress or by the States. It is therefore vital that the standards for judging obscenity safeguard the protection of freedom of speech and press for material which does not treat sex in a manner appealing to prurient interest.

The early leading standard of obscenity allowed material to be judged merely by the effect of an isolated excerpt upon particularly susceptible persons. *Regina v. Hicklin.* [L]ater decisions have rejected it and substituted this test: whether to the average person, applying contemporary community standards, the dominant theme of the material taken as a whole appeals to prurient interest. The *Hicklin* test, judging obscenity by the effect of isolated passages upon the most susceptible persons, might well encompass material legitimately treating with sex, and so it must be rejected as unconstitutionally restrictive of the freedoms of speech and press. On the other hand, the substituted standard provides safeguards adequate to withstand the charge of constitutional infirmity.

The judgments are affirmed.

TIMES FILM CORPORATION v. CITY OF CHICAGO, 365 U.S. 43 (1961)

Abridgment of Dissenting Opinion of Mr. Chief Justice Warren, with whom Mr. Justice Black, Mr. Justice Douglas and Mr. Justice Brennan joined.

I cannot agree with either the conclusion reached by the Court or with the reasons advanced for its support. To me, this case clearly presents the question of our approval of unlimited censorship of motion pictures before exhibition through a system of administrative licensing. Moreover, the decision presents a real danger of eventual censorship for every form of communication, be it newspapers, journals, books, magazines, television, radio or public speeches. The Court purports to leave these questions for another day, but I am aware of no constitutional principle which permits us to hold that the communication of ideas through one medium may be censored while other media are immune. Of course each medium presents its own peculiar problems, but they are not of the kind which would authorize the censorship of one form of communication and not others. I submit that in arriving at its decision the Court has interpreted our cases contrary to the intention at the time of their rendition and, in exalting the censor of motion pictures, has endangered the First and Fourteenth Amendment rights of all others engaged in the dissemination of ideas.

The vice of censorship through licensing and, more generally, the particular evil of previous restraint on the right of free speech have many times been recognized when this Court has carefully distinguished between laws establishing sundry systems of previous restraint on the right of free speech and penal laws imposing subsequent punishment on utterances and activities not within the ambit of the First Amendment's protection.

Examination of the background and circumstances leading to the adoption of the First Amendment reveals the basis for the Court's steadfast observance of the proscription of licensing, censorship and previous restraint of speech. Such inquiry often begins with Blackstone's assertion: "The liberty of the press is indeed essential to the nature of a free state; but this consists in laying no previous restraint upon publications, and not in freedom from censure for criminal matter when published."

Let it be completely clear what the Court's decision does. It gives official license to the censor, approving a grant of power to city officials to prevent the showing of any moving picture these officials deem unworthy of a license. It thus gives formal sanction to censorship in its purest and most far-reaching form, to a classical plan of licensing that, in our country, most closely approaches the English licensing laws of the seventeenth century which were commonly used to suppress dissent in the mother country and in the colonies.

By its decision, the Court gives its assent to unlimited censorship of moving pictures through a licensing system, despite the fact that Chicago has chosen this most objectionable course to attain its goals without any apparent attempt to devise other means so as not to intrude on the constitutionally protected liberties of speech and press.

The case of *Grosjean v. American Press Co.,* . . . provides . . . [a] forceful illustration. The Court held there that a license tax of two percent on the gross receipts from advertising of newspapers and periodicals having a circulation of over 20,000 a week was a form of prior restraint and therefore invalid. Certainly this would seem much less an infringement on the liberties of speech and press protected by the First and Fourteenth Amendments than the classic system of censorship we now have before us.

A revelation of the extent to which censorship has recently been used in this country is indeed astonishing. The Chicago licensors have banned newsreel films of Chicago policemen shooting at labor pickets and have ordered the deletion of a scene depicting the birth of a buffalo in Walt Disney's *Vanishing Prairie.* . . . Before World War II, the Chicago censor denied licenses to a number of films portraying and criticizing life in Nazi Germany including the March of Time's *Inside Nazi Germany.* . . . Recently, Chicago refused to issue a permit for the exhibition of the motion picture *Anatomy of a Murder* based upon the best-selling novel of the same title, because it found the use of the words "rape" and "contraceptive" to be objectionable. . . . The Memphis censors banned *The Southerner* which dealt with poverty among tenant farmers because "it reflects on the south." *Brewster's Millions,* an innocuous comedy of fifty years ago, was recently forbidden in Memphis because the radio and film character Rochester, a Negro, was deemed "too familiar." . . . Maryland censors restricted a Polish documentary film on the basis that it failed to present a true picture of modern Poland. . . . *No Way Out,* the story of a Negro doctor's struggle against race prejudice, was banned by the Chicago censor on the ground that "there's a possibility it could cause trouble." The principal objection to the film was that the conclusion showed no reconciliation between blacks and whites. The ban was lifted after a storm of protest and later deletion of a scene showing Negroes and whites arming for a gang fight. . . . Memphis banned *Curley* because it contained scenes of white and Negro children in school together. . . . Atlanta barred *Lost Boundaries,* the story of a Negro physician and his family who "passed" for white, on the ground that the exhibition of said picture "will adversely affect the peace, morals and good order" in the city. . . . The New York censors banned *Damaged Lives,* a film dealing with venereal disease, although it treated a difficult theme with dignity and had the sponsorship of the American Social Hygiene Society. The picture of Lenin's tomb bearing the inscription "Religion is the opiate of the people" was excised from *Potemkin.* From *Joan of Arc* the Maryland board eliminated Joan's exclamation as she stood at the stake: "Oh, God, why hast thou forsaken me?" and from *Idiot's Delight,* the sentence: "We, the workers of the world, will take care of that." *Professor Mamlock* was produced in Russia and portrayed the persecution of the Jews by Nazis. The Ohio censors condemned it as "harmful" and calculated to "stir up hatred and ill will and gain nothing." It was released only after substantial deletions were made. The police refused to permit its showing in Providence, Rhode Island, on the ground that it was communistic propaganda. *Millions of Us,* a strong union propaganda film, encountered trouble in a number of jurisdictions. *Spanish Earth,* a pro-Loyalist documentary picture, was banned by the board in Pennsylvania. . . . During the year ending June 30, 1938, the New York board censored, in one way or another, over five percent of the moving pictures it reviewed. . . . Charlie Chaplin's satire on Hitler, *The Great Dictator,* was banned in Chicago, apparently out of deference to its large German population. . . . Ohio and Kansas banned newsreels considered pro labor. Kansas ordered a speech by Senator Wheeler opposing the bill for enlarging the Supreme Court to be cut from the *March of Time* as "partisan and biased." . . . An early version of *Carmen* was condemned on several different grounds. The Ohio censor objected because cigarette-girls smoked cigarettes in public. . . .

This is the regimen to which the Court holds that all films must be submitted. . . . It does not require an active imagination to conceive of the quantum of ideas that will surely be suppressed.

Freedom of speech and freedom of the press are further endangered by this "most effective" means for confinement of ideas. It is axiomatic that the stroke of the censor's pen or the cut of his scissors will be a less contemplated decision than will be the prosecutor's determination to prepare a criminal indictment. The standards of proof, the judicial safeguards afforded a criminal defendant and the consequences of bringing such charges will all provoke the mature deliberation of the prosecutor. None of these hinder the quick judgment of the censor, the speedy determination to suppress.

XVII

LABOR UNIONS AND PICKETING

Of prime importance are the rights of working people to join in labor unions, to bargain collectively for working conditions, and, if necessary, to strike against their employers and use picketing to make their grievances known to the general public.

Prior to the Industrial Revolution, most of the attempts of labor to organize in unions, as distinguished from the earlier craft guilds, were deemed illegal conspiracies and were terminated by injunction or penal action. Legitimization of unions was gradual and progressive so that by the mid-nineteenth century, the right of labor to organize and bargain collectively was generally established, and early in this century, legislation was adopted guaranteeing these rights.

During the Roosevelt New Deal era, Congress passed the National Labor Relations Act to protect these rights for workers in interstate industries under its power to regulate interstate commerce. Employers against whom a strike would even indirectly interfere with interstate industry are subject to this Federal act.

An individual may leave his employment whenever he desires. Any interference with this absolute right is a violation of the Thirteenth Amendment prohibition of involuntary servitude. A strike, however, is not the result of individual decision to leave employment, it is a concerted group action to bring economic pressure upon an employer. As Justice Brandeis once observed, "[N]either the common law nor the Fourteenth Amendment confers the absolute right to strike." [*Dorchy v. Kansas,* 272 U.S. 306 (1926)] The difficulty is, of course, in where to draw the line, as without the power to strike the right of workers to organize is considerably devalued.

Under the Taft-Hartley Act, strikes affecting interstate commerce that are designed to achieve purposes other than the settlement of labor grievances may be prohibited. Thus, a strike may be enjoined if its object is a secondary boycott or if it is an attempt to coerce an employer into recognizing or bargaining with a union which has not been certified as the employees' representative by the National Labor Relations Board. [29 U.S.C. Sect. 158 (4)] Pursuant to the same Act, a strike may be temporarily enjoined when a Presidential fact finding board finds that it imperils the national health or safety. When the injunction is issued, the parties must negotiate in good faith under the supervision of the Board. After sixty days elapse, the Board must submit the final offer of the employer to a secret vote of the employees. Should the employees reject the offer, the injunction must be vacated and the strike may then continue. [29 U.S.C. Sects. 176–180]

In the Landrum-Griffin Act of 1959, which modified the Taft-Hartley Act, Congress added further restrictions on the economic activities of labor unions. The act also imposed restrictions on the internal operation of unions which trade unionists opposed as governmental interference. In effect, however, the act created a new measure of protection for the civil liberties of the union members.

Some States have statutes prohibiting strikes by Civil Service employees and by workers in fields serving an essential public need. In New York, for example, where Civil Service employees may organize in unions, they are forbidden to strike. However, in the absence of such statutory prohibition, public inconvenience, although substantial, is insufficient cause to enjoin a strike.

The States may also regulate the conduct of a strike to prevent violence or some other unlawful act. Included in such unlawful acts are sit-down strikes, "quickie" strikes (that is, stoppages of work for short successive periods without notice to the employer), and interference with production by means other than leaving the employer's premises. [*International Union v. Wisconsin,* 336 U.S. 245 (1949)]

The right to picket raises many of the same problems that are raised by the right to strike. At one time it was held that picketing was an absolute right because it was a form of communication protected by the First Amendment. [*Thornhill v. Alabama,* 310 U.S. 88 (1940)] It is now recognized that picketing involves more than communication and that it is not an absolute right. Justice Douglas said that picketing was ". . . more than free speech, since it involves patrol of the particular locality and since the very presence of the picket line may induce action of one kind or another, quite irrespective of the ideas being disseminated." [*Bakery Drivers Local v. Wohl,* 315 U.S. 769 (1942)]

If the ends sought by picketing are lawful and if the means by which it is conducted are truthful and lawful, the right to picket an employer's establishment cannot be taken away. Similarly, picketing may be conducted for social protest not involving a labor dispute. However, when picketing leads to violence or the destruction of property or would clearly lead to such unsocial action if permitted to continue, a State may enjoin the picketing. [*Milk Wagon Drivers Union v. Meadowmoor Dairies,* 312 U.S. 287 (1941)] When picketing is intended to induce an employer or another to take action which is illegal, it may be stopped. A Missouri court's injunction was sustained where the purpose of the picketing was to prevent a wholesaler from selling to non-union peddlers, an act which would have violated Missouri's antitrust laws. [*Giboney v. Empire Storage and Ice Co.,* 336 U.S. 490 (1949)] Similarly, a State may enjoin picketing by a union which had previously been unsuccessful in its attempt to organize the employees of the picketed business. [*International Brotherhood of Teamsters v. Vogt;* the Court's opinion, in abridgment, is at page 147.] And when picketing for the purpose of communicating social protest seeks an objective subversive of established State policy, it too may be enjoined. Thus, when pickets attempted to coerce the management of a business into hiring Negro employees in proportion to the number of its colored customers, the picketing was halted. The objective sought was subversive of the State's policy of equal treatment in employment practices, regardless of race. [*Hughes v. Superior Court,* 339 U.S. 460 (1950); see also *Cassell v. Texas;* the Court's opinion is at page 45.]

At one time employers attempted to avoid collective bargaining by entering into so-called "yellow dog contracts" with their employees. These were agreements by the employee not to become a member of a union during the period of his employment. State statutes making it a crime to require such contracts as a condition of employment were at first held to be unconstitutional as interfering with the right to freely contract. But subsequent legislation declaring such contracts unenforceable by judicial action was held not to violate any constitutional rights of employers.

Because of the remarkable growth of the labor union movement, some States now claim substantive evil in the "closed shop" agreement by which the employer agrees to hire none but union members. In consequence, twenty States have enacted so-called "right to work" laws which provide that union membership cannot be made a prerequisite to employment. These laws have been held constitutional, on the ground that they prevent discrimination against persons not union members. [*A.F.L. v. American Sash,* 335 U.S. 538 (1949)] The Court said the right to assemble was not a guaranty that those who refuse to join the assembly shall be barred from employment.

Proponents in the various States of these "right to work" laws are the National Association of Manufacturers, the United States Chamber of Commerce, and open shop employers. While the slogan "right to work" sounds fair and equitable, in reality these laws protect a right to work under conditions unilaterally established by employers. It is significant that all of the States which have "right to work" laws, with the exception of Indiana, are not in the industrialized part of the country but in the agricultural southern and border States. In the 1959 elections, California, Ohio, and Kansas had proposals for "right to work" laws on referendum ballots. The proposals were defeated in California and Ohio but adopted in Kansas. There was no State action for adoption or repeal of the laws in 1960 or 1961. However, the A.F.L.–C.I.O. is engaged in an intensive effort in many of the States for repeal of the "right to work" laws.

INTERNATIONAL BROTHERHOOD OF TEAMSTERS v. VOGT, 354 U.S. 284 (1957)

Abridgment of Mr. Justice Frankfurter's Opinion for the Court. (Mr. Justice Douglas dissented in an opinion in which Mr. Chief Justice Warren and Mr. Justice Black concurred. Mr. Justice Whittaker took no part.)

This is one more in the long series of cases in which this Court has been required to consider the limits imposed by the Fourteenth Amendment on the power of a State to enjoin picketing. Respondent owns and operates a gravel pit in Wisconsin, where it employs 15 to 20 men. Petitioner unions sought unsuccessfully to induce some of respondent's employees to join the unions and commenced to picket the entrance to respondent's place of business with signs reading, "The men on this job are not 100% affiliated with the A.F.L." In consequence, drivers of several trucking companies refused to deliver and haul goods to and from respondent's plant, causing substantial damage to respondent. Respondent thereupon sought an injunction to restrain the picketing.

[The trial court] held that by virtue of Wis. Stat. §103.535, prohibiting picketing in the absence of a "labor dispute," the petitioners must be enjoined.

It is inherent in the concept embodied in the Due Process Clause that its scope be determined by a "gradual process of judicial inclusion and exclusion." It is not too surprising that the response of States—legislative and judicial—to use of the injunction in labor controversies should have given rise to a series of adjudications in this Court relating to the limitations on state action contained in the provisions of the Due Process Clause of the Fourteenth Amendment. It is also not too surprising that examination of these adjudications should disclose an evolving, not a static, course of decision.

Apart from remedying the abuses of the injunction in this general type of ligitation, legislatures and courts began to find in one of the aims of picketing an aspect of communication. This view came to the fore in *Senn v. Tile Layers Union,* where the Court held that the Fourteenth Amendment did not prohibit Wisconsin from authorizing peaceful stranger picketing by a union that was attempting to unionize a shop and to induce an employer to refrain from working in his business as a laborer.

[T]hree years later, in passing on a restrictive instead of a permissive state statute, the Court made sweeping pronouncements about the right to picket in holding unconstitutional a statute that had been applied to ban all picketing, with "no exceptions based upon either the number of persons engaged in the proscribed activity, the peaceful character of their demeanor, the nature of their dispute with an employer, or the restrained character and the accurateness of the terminology used in notifying the public of the facts of the dispute." *Thornhill v. Alabama.* As the statute dealt at large with all picketing, so the Court broadly assimilated peaceful picketing in general to freedom of speech, and as such protected against abridgement by the Fourteenth Amendment.

These principles were applied by the Court to hold unconstitutional an injunction against peaceful picketing, based on a State's common-law policy against picketing when there was no immediate dispute between employer and employee. On the same day, however, the Court upheld a generalized injunction against picketing where there had been violence because "it could justifiably be concluded that the momentum of fear generated by past violence would survive even though future picketing might be wholly peaceful."

Cases reached the Court in which a State had designed a remedy to meet a specific situation or to accomplish a particular social policy. These cases made manifest that picketing, even though "peaceful," involved more than just communication of ideas and could not be immune from all state regulation. "Picketing by an organized group is more than free speech, since it involves patrol of a particular locality and since the very presence of a picket line may induce action of one kind or another, quite irrespective of the nature of the ideas which are being disseminated."

These cases required the Court to review a choice made by two States between the competing interests of unions, employers, their employees, and the public at large. In the *Ritter's Cafe* case, Texas had enjoined as a violation of its antitrust law picketing of a restaurant by unions to bring pressure on its owner with respect to the use of nonunion labor by a contractor of the restaurant owner in the construction of a building having nothing to do with the restaurant. The Court held that Texas could, consistent with the Fourteenth Amendment, insulate from the dispute a neutral establishment that industrially had no connection with it. This type of picketing certainly involved little, if any, "communication."

In *Hughes v. Superior Court*, the Court held that the Fourteenth

Amendment did not bar use of the injunction to prohibit picketing of a place of business solely to secure compliance with a demand that its employees be hired in percentage to the racial origin of its customers. "We cannot construe the Due Process Clause as precluding California from securing respect for its policy against involuntary employment on racial lines by prohibiting systematic picketing that would subvert such policy."

On the same day, the Court decided that a State was not restrained by the Fourteenth Amendment from enjoining picketing of a business, conducted by the owner himself without employees, in order to secure compliance with a demand to become a union shop.

A third case, *Building Service Employees v. Gazzam,* was decided the same day. Following an unsuccessful attempt at unionization of a small hotel . . . the union begin to picket the hotel with signs stating that the owner was unfair to organized labor. The State, finding that the object of the picketing was in violation of its statutory policy against employer coercion of employees' choice of bargaining representative, enjoined picketing for such purpose. This Court affirmed.

This series of cases, then, established a broad field in which a State, in enforcing some public policy, whether of its criminal or its civil law, and whether announced by its legislature or its courts, could constitutionally enjoin peaceful picketing aimed at preventing effectuation of that policy.

Of course, the mere fact that there is "picketing" does not automatically justify its restraint without an investigation into its conduct and purposes. State courts, no more than state legislatures, can enact blanket prohibitions against picketing. In this case, the circumstances set forth in the opinion of the Wisconsin Supreme Court afford a rational basis for the inference it drew concerning the purpose of the picketing. No question was raised here concerning the breadth of the injunction, but of course its terms must be read in the light of the opinion of the Wisconsin Supreme Court, which justified it on the ground that the picketing was for the purpose of coercing the employer to coerce his employees.

Therefore, . . . we affirm.

Appendices

■ ■

A

THE BILL OF RIGHTS IN THE UNITED STATES CONSTITUTION

The Ten Original Amendments

THE FIRST AMENDMENT. Congress shall make no law respecting an establishment of religion, or prohibiting the free exercise thereof; or abridging the freedom of speech, or of the press; or the right of the people peaceably to assemble, and to petition the Government for a redress of grievances.

THE SECOND AMENDMENT. A well regulated Militia, being necessary to the security of a free State, the right of the people to keep and bear Arms, shall not be infringed.

THE THIRD AMENDMENT. No Soldier shall, in time of peace, be quartered in any house, without the consent of the Owner, nor in time of war, but in a manner to be prescribed by law.

THE FOURTH AMENDMENT. The right of the people to be secure in their persons, houses, papers, and effects, against unreasonable searches and seizures, shall not be violated, and no Warrants shall issue, but upon probable cause, supported by Oath or affirmation, and particularly describing the place to be searched, and the persons or things to be seized.

THE FIFTH AMENDMENT. No person shall be held to answer for a capital, or otherwise infamous crime, unless on a presentment or indictment of a Grand Jury, except in cases arising in the land or naval forces, or in the Militia, when in actual service in time of War or public danger; nor shall any person be subject for the same offence to be twice put in jeopardy of life or limb; nor shall be compelled in any criminal case to be a witness against himself, nor be deprived of life, liberty, or property, without due process of law; nor shall private property be taken for public use, without just compensation.

THE SIXTH AMENDMENT. In all criminal prosecutions, the accused shall enjoy the right to a speedy and public trial, by an impartial jury of the State and district wherein the crime shall have been committed, which district shall have been previously ascertained by law, and to be informed of the nature and cause of the accusation; to be confronted with the witnesses against him; to have compulsory process for obtaining witnesses in his favor, and to have the Assistance of Counsel for his defence.

THE SEVENTH AMENDMENT. In Suits at common law, where the value in controversy shall exceed twenty dollars, the right of trial by jury shall be preserved, and no fact tried by a jury, shall be otherwise re-examined in any Court of the United States, than according to the rules of the common law.

THE EIGHTH AMENDMENT. Excessive bail shall not be required, nor excessive fines imposed, nor cruel and unusual punishments inflicted.

THE NINTH AMENDMENT. The enumeration in the Constitution, of certain rights, shall not be construed to deny or disparage others retained by the people.

THE TENTH AMENDMENT. The powers not delegated to the United States by the Constitution, nor prohibited by it to the States, are reserved to the States respectively, or to the people.

Additional Amendments Dealing With Personal Liberty*

THE THIRTEENTH AMENDMENT. Neither slavery nor involuntary servitude, except as a punishment for crime whereof the party shall have been duly convicted, shall exist within the United States, or any place subject to their jurisdiction.

THE FOURTEENTH AMENDMENT. All persons born or naturalized in the United States, and subject to the jurisdiction thereof, are citizens of the United States and of the State wherein they reside. No State shall make or enforce any law which shall abridge the privileges or immunities of citizens of the United States; nor

---

* Enforcement and other clauses not dealing directly with personal liberties are omitted.

shall any State deprive any person of life, liberty, or property, without due process of law; nor deny to any person within its jurisdiction the equal protection of the laws.

THE FIFTEENTH AMENDMENT. The right of citizens of the United States to vote shall not be denied or abridged by the United States or by any State on account of race, color, or previous condition of servitude.

THE NINETEENTH AMENDMENT. The right of citizens of the United States to vote shall not be denied or abridged by the United States or by any State on account of sex.

Provisions in the Original Constitution Dealing With Personal Liberty*

ARTICLE I. *Section 9.* . . . The Privilege of the Writ of Habeas Corpus shall not be suspended, unless when in Cases of Rebellion or Invasion the public Safety may require it.

No Bill of Attainder or ex post facto Law shall be passed.

Section 10. No State shall . . . pass any Bill of Attainder, ex post facto Law . . .

ARTICLE III. *Section 2.* . . . The Trial of all Crimes . . . shall be by Jury . . .

Section 3. Treason against the United States, shall consist only in levying War against them, or in adhering to their Enemies . . .

ARTICLE IV. *Section 2.* The Citizens of each State shall be entitled to all Privileges and Immunities of Citizens in the several States.

ARTICLE VI. . . . no religious Test shall ever be required as a Qualification to any Office or public Trust under the United States.

---

* Clauses not dealing directly with personal liberties are omitted.

B

THE DECLARATION OF INDEPENDENCE

In Congress, July 4, 1776. The unanimous Declaration of the thirteen united States of America,

When in the course of human events it becomes necessary for one people to dissolve the political bands which have connected them with another, and to assume among the powers of the earth, the separate and equal station to which the Laws of Nature and of Nature's God entitle them, a decent respect to the opinions of mankind requires that they should declare the causes which impel them to the separation.

We hold these truths to be self-evident, that all men are created equal, that they are endowed by their Creator with certain unalienable Rights, that among these are Life, Liberty and the pursuit of Happiness. That to secure these rights, Governments are instituted among Men, deriving their just powers from the consent of the governed, That whenever any Form of Government becomes destructive of these ends, it is the Right of the People to alter or to abolish it, and to institute new Government, laying its foundation on such principles and organizing its powers in such form, as to them shall seem most likely to effect their Safety and Happiness. Prudence, indeed, will dictate that Governments long established should not be changed for light and transient causes; and accordingly all experience hath shewn, that mankind are more disposed to suffer, while evils are sufferable, than to right themselves by abolishing the forms to which they are accustomed. But when a long train of abuses and usurpations, pursuing invariably the same Object evinces a design to reduce them under absolute Despotism, it is their right, it is their duty, to throw off such Government, and to provide new Guards for their future security. Such has been the patient sufferance of these Colonies; and such is now the necessity which constrains them to alter their former Systems of Government. The history of the present King of Great Britain is a history of repeated injuries and usurpations, all having in direct object the establishment of an absolute Tyranny over these States. To prove this, let Facts be submitted to a candid world.

He has refused his Assent to Laws, the most wholesome and necessary for the public good.

He has forbidden his Governors to pass Laws of immediate and pressing importance, unless suspended in their operation till his Assent should be obtained; and when so suspended, he has utterly neglected to attend to them.

He has refused to pass other Laws for the accommodation of large districts of people, unless those people would relinquish the right of Representation in the Legislature, a right inestimable to them and formidable to tyrants only.

He has called together legislative bodies at places unusual, uncomfortable, and distant from the depository of their public Records, for the sole purpose of fatiguing them into compliance with his measures.

He has dissolved Representative Houses repeatedly, for, opposing with manly firmness his invasions on the rights of the people.

He has refused for a long time, after such dissolutions, to cause others to be elected; whereby the Legislative powers, incapable of Annihilation, have returned to the People at large for their exercise; the State remaining in the mean time exposed to all the dangers of invasion from without, and convulsions within.

He has endeavoured to prevent the population of these States; for that purpose obstructing the Laws for Naturalization of Foreigners; refusing to pass others to encourage their migration hither, and raising the conditions of new Appropriations of Lands.

He has obstructed the Administration of Justice, by refusing his Assent to Laws for establishing Judiciary powers.

He has made Judges dependent on his Will alone, for the tenure of their offices, and the amount and payment of their salaries.

He has erected a multitude of New Offices, and sent hither swarms of Officers to harass our people, and eat out their substance.

He has kept among us, in time of peace, Standing Armies without the Consent of our legislatures.

He has affected to render the Military independent of and superior to the Civil power.

He has combined with others to subject us to a jurisdiction foreign to our constitution, and unacknowledged by our laws; giving his Assent to their Acts of pretended Legislation:

For quartering large bodies of armed troops among us:

For protecting them, by a mock Trial, from punishment for any Murders which they should commit on the Inhabitants of these States:

For cutting off our Trade with all parts of the world:

For imposing taxes on us without our Consent:

For depriving us in many cases, of the benefits of Trial by Jury:

For transporting us beyond Seas to be tried for pretended offences:

For abolishing the free System of English Laws in a neighbouring Province, establishing therein an Arbitrary government, and enlarging its Boundaries so as to render it at once an example and fit instrument for introducing the same absolute rule into these Colonies:

For taking away our Charters, abolishing our most valuable Laws, and altering fundamentally the Forms of our Governments:

For suspending our own Legislatures and declaring themselves invested with power to legislate for us in all cases whatsoever.

He has abdicated Government here, by declaring us out of his Protection and waging War against us.

He has plundered our seas, ravaged our Coasts, burnt our towns, and destroyed the lives of our people.

He is at this time transporting large Armies of foreign Mercenaries to compleat the works of death, desolation and tyranny, already begun with circumstances of Cruelty & perfidy scarcely paralleled in the most barbarous ages, and totally unworthy the Head of a civilized nation.

He has constrained our fellow Citizens taken Captive on the high Seas to bear Arms against their Country, to become the executioners of their friends and Brethren, or to fall themselves by their Hands.

He has excited domestic insurrections amongst us, and has endeavoured to bring on the inhabitants of our frontiers, the merciless Indian Savages, whose known rule of warfare, is an undistinguished destruction of all ages, sexes and conditions.

In every stage of these Oppressions We have Petitioned for Redress in the most humble terms: Our repeated Petitions have been answered only by repeated injury. A Prince, whose character is thus marked by every act which may define a Tyrant, is unfit to be the ruler of a free people.

Nor have We been wanting in attentions to our Brittish brethren. We have warned them from time to time of attempts by their legislature to extend an unwarrantable jurisdiction over us. We have reminded them of the circumstances of our emigration and settlement here. We have appealed to their native justice and magnanimity, and we have conjured them by the ties of our common kindred to disavow these usurpations, which would inevitably interrupt our connections and correspondence. They too have been deaf to the voice of justice and of consanguinity. We must, therefore, acquiesce in the necessity, which denounces our Separation, and hold them, as we hold the rest of mankind, Enemies in War, in Peace Friends.

We, therefore, the Representatives of the united States of America, in General Congress, Assembled, appealing to the Supreme Judge of the world for the rectitude of our intentions, do, in the Name, and by Authority of the good People of these Colonies, solemnly publish and declare, That these United Colonies are, and of Right ought to be Free and Independent States; that they are Absolved from all Allegiance to the British Crown, and that all political connection between them and the

State of Great Britain, is and ought to be totally dissolved; and that as Free and Independent States, they have full Power to levy War, conclude Peace, contract Alliances, establish Commerce, and to do all other Acts and Things which Independent States may of right do. And for the support of this Declaration, with a firm reliance on the protection of Divine Providence, we mutually pledge to each other our Lives, our Fortunes and our sacred Honor.

C

THE CANADIAN BILL OF RIGHTS

1. It is hereby recognized and declared that in Canada there have existed and shall continue to exist without discrimination by reason of race, national origin, colour, religion or sex, the following human rights and fundamental freedoms, namely,

(a) the right of the individual to life, liberty, security of the person and enjoyment of property, and the right not to be deprived thereof except by due process of law;
(b) the right of the individual to equality before the law and the protection of the law;
(c) freedom of religion;
(d) freedom of speech;
(e) freedom of assembly and association; and
(f) freedom of the press.

2. Every law of Canada shall, unless it is expressly declared by an Act of the Parliament of Canada that it shall operate notwithstanding the *Canadian Bill of Rights*, be so construed and applied as not to abrogate, abridge or infringe or to authorize the abrogation, abridgment or infringement of any of the rights or freedoms herein recognized and declared, and in particular, no law of Canada shall be construed or applied so as to

(a) authorize or effect the arbitrary detention, imprisonment or exile of any person;
(b) impose or authorize the imposition of cruel and unusual treatment or punishment;
(c) deprive a person who has been arrested or detained
(i) of the right to be informed promptly of the reason for his arrest or detention,
(ii) of the right to retain and instruct counsel without delay, or

      (iii) of the remedy by way of *habeas corpus* for the determination of the validity of his detention and for his release if the detention is not lawful;

(d) authorize a court, tribunal, commission, board or other authority to compel a person to give evidence if he is denied counsel, protection against self crimination or other constitutional safeguards;

(e) deprive a person of the right to a fair hearing in accordance with the principles of fundamental justice for the determination of his rights and obligations;

(f) deprive a person charged with a criminal offense of the right to be presumed innocent until proved guilty according to law in a fair and public hearing by an independent and impartial tribunal, or of the right to reasonable bail without just cause; or

(g) deprive a person of the right to the assistance of an interpreter in any proceedings in which he is involved or in which he is a party or a witness, before a court, commission, board or other tribunal, if he does not understand or speak the language in which such proceedings are conducted.

3. The Minister of Justice shall, in accordance with such regulations as may be prescribed by the Governor in Council, examine every proposed regulation submitted in draft form to the Clerk of the Privy Council pursuant to the *Regulations Act* and every Bill introduced in or presented to the House of Commons, in order to ascertain whether any of the provisions thereof are inconsistent with the purposes and provisions of this Part and he shall report any such inconsistency to the House of Commons at the first convenient opportunity.

D

THE UNIVERSAL DECLARATION OF HUMAN RIGHTS

INTRODUCTORY COMMENT. On December 10, 1948 the General Assembly of the United Nations adopted and proclaimed the Universal Declaration of Human Rights. Following this historic act the Assembly called upon all member states to publicize the text of the Declaration and "to cause it to be disseminated, displayed, read and expounded principally in schools and other educational institutions, without distinction based on the political status of countries or territories."

The Declaration has become widely known; it has been translated into some fifty languages and has influenced international agreements, treaties, new national constitutions, legislation and court decisions in many countries, and the rights of United Nations officials in their relationship to the Organization. But the Declaration does not have the force of a treaty or covenant. The Commission on Human Rights is engaged in drafting covenants to implement the Declaration. Whether the 103 present member states will all accept the covenants is questionable. When the Declaration was adopted in 1948, the United States and 47 other member states voted for it; there were no votes in opposition, but the Soviet Union, Ukrainian Republic, Byelorussia, Poland, Czechoslovakia, Yugoslavia, Saudi Arabia, and the Union of South Africa abstained from voting. The 47 states which have been admitted to the United Nations since December 10, 1948 have not voted on the Declaration as no provision was made for subsequent acceptances.

A. D. W.

Preamble

WHEREAS recognition of the inherent dignity of the equal and inalienable rights of all members of the human family is the foundation of freedom, justice and peace in the world,

WHEREAS disregard and contempt for human rights have resulted in barbarous acts which have outraged the conscience of mankind, and the advent of a world in which human beings shall enjoy freedom of speech and belief and freedom from fear and want has been proclaimed as the highest aspiration of the common people,

WHEREAS it is essential, if man is not to be compelled to have recourse, as a last resort, to rebellion against tyranny and oppression, that human rights should be protected by the rule of law,

WHEREAS it is essential to promote the development of friendly relations between nations,

WHEREAS the peoples of the United Nations have in the Charter reaffirmed their faith in fundamental human rights, in the dignity and worth of the human person and in the equal rights of men and women and have determined to promote social progress and better standards of life in larger freedom,

WHEREAS Member States have pledged themselves to achieve, in co-operation with the United Nations, the promotion of universal respect for and observance of human rights and fundamental freedoms,

WHEREAS a common understanding of these rights and freedoms is of the greatest importance for the full realisation of this pledge,

Now THEREFORE The General Assembly Proclaims this Universal Declaration of Human Rights as a common standard of achievement for all peoples and all nations, to the end that every individual and every organ of society, keeping this Declaration constantly in mind, shall strive by teaching and education to promote respect for these rights and freedoms and by progressive measures, national and international, to secure their universal and effective recognition and observance, both among the peoples of Member States themselves and among the peoples of territories under their jurisdiction.

ARTICLE 1. All human beings are born free and equal in dignity and rights. They are endowed with reason and conscience and should act towards one another in a spirit of brotherhood.

ARTICLE 2. Everyone is entitled to all the rights and freedoms set forth in this Declaration, without distinction of any kind, such as race, colour, sex, language, religion, political or other opinion, national or social origin, property, birth or other status. Furthermore, no distinction shall be made on the basis of the political, jurisdictional or international status of the country or territory to which a person belongs, whether it be independent, trust, non-self-governing or under any other limitation of sovereignty.

ARTICLE 3. Everyone has the right to life, liberty and security of person.

ARTICLE 4. No one shall be held in slavery or servitude; slavery and the slave trade shall be prohibited in all their forms.

ARTICLE 5. No one shall be subjected to torture or to cruel, inhuman or degrading treatment or punishment.

ARTICLE 6. Everyone has the right to recognition everywhere as a person before the law.

ARTICLE 7. All are equal before the law and are entitled without any discrimination to equal protection of the law. All are entitled to equal protection against any discrimination in violation of this Declaration and against any incitement to such discrimination.

ARTICLE 8. Everyone has the right to an effective remedy by the competent national tribunals for acts violating the fundamental rights granted him by the constitution or by law.

ARTICLE 9. No one shall be subjected to arbitrary arrest, detention or exile.

ARTICLE 10. Everyone is entitled in full equality to a fair and public hearing by an independent and impartial tribunal, in the determination of his rights and obligations and of any criminal charge against him.

ARTICLE 11. (1) Everyone charged with a penal offence has the right to be presumed innocent until proved guilty according to law in a public trial at which he has had all the guarantees necessary for his defence.

(2) No one shall be held guilty of any penal offence on account of any act or omission which did not constitute a penal offence, under national or international law, at the time when it was committed. Nor shall a heavier penalty be imposed than the one that was applicable at the time the penal offence was committed.

ARTICLE 12. No one shall be subjected to arbitrary interference with his privacy, family, home or correspondence, nor to attacks upon his honour and reputation. Everyone has the right to the protection of the law against such interference or attacks.

ARTICLE 13. (1) Everyone has the right to freedom of movement and residence within the borders of each state.

(2) Everyone has the right to leave any country, including his own, and to return to his country.

ARTICLE 14. (1) Everyone has the right to seek and to enjoy in other countries asylum from persecution.

(2) This right may not be invoked in the case of prosecutions genuinely arising from non-political crimes or from acts contrary to the purposes and principles of the United Nations.

ARTICLE 15. (1) Everyone has the right to a nationality.

(2) No one shall be arbitrarily deprived of his nationality nor denied the right to change his nationality.

ARTICLE 16. (1) Men and women of full age, without any limitation due to race, nationality or religion, have the right to marry and to found a family. They are entitled to equal rights as to marriage, during marriage and at its dissolution.

(2) Marriage shall be entered into only with the free and full consent of the intending spouses.

(3) The family is the natural and fundamental group unit of society and is entitled to protection by society and the State.

ARTICLE 17. (1) Everyone has the right to own property alone as well as in association with others.

(2) No one shall be arbitrarily deprived of his property.

ARTICLE 18. Everyone has the right to freedom of thought, conscience and religion; this right includes freedom to change his religion or belief, and freedom, either alone or in community with others and in public or private, to manifest his religion or belief in teaching, practice, worship and observance.

ARTICLE 19. Everyone has the right to freedom of opinion and expression; this right includes freedom to hold opinions without interference and to seek, receive and impart information and ideas through any media and regardless of frontiers.

ARTICLE 20. (1) Everyone has the right to freedom of peaceful assembly and association.

(2) No one may be compelled to belong to an association.

ARTICLE 21. (1) Everyone has the right to take part in the government of his country, directly or through freely chosen representatives.

(2) Everyone has the right of equal access to public service in his country.

(3) The will of the people shall be the basis of the authority of government; this will shall be expressed in periodic and genuine elections which shall be by universal and equal suffrage and shall be held by secret vote or by equivalent free voting procedures.

ARTICLE 22. Everyone, as a member of society, has the right to social security and is entitled to realisation, through national effort and international co-operation and in accordance with the organisation and resources of each State, of the economic, social and cultural rights indispensable for his dignity and the free development of his personality.

ARTICLE 23. (1) Everyone has the right to work, to free choice of employment, to just and favourable conditions of work and to protection against unemployment.

(2) Everyone, without any discrimination, has the right to equal pay for equal work.

(3) Everyone who works has the right to just and favourable remuneration insuring for himself and his family an existence worthy of human dignity, and supplemented, if necessary, by other means of social protection.

(4) Everyone has the right to form and to join trade unions for the protection of his interests.

ARTICLE 24. Everyone has the right to rest and leisure, including reasonable limitation of working hours and periodic holidays with pay.

ARTICLE 25. (1) Everyone has the right to a standard of living adequate for the health and well-being of himself and of his family, including food, clothing, housing, and medical care and necessary social services, and the right to security in the event of unemployment, sickness, disability, widowhood, old age or other lack of livelihood in circumstances beyond his control.

(2) Motherhood and childhood are entitled to special care and assistance. All children, whether born in or out of wedlock, shall enjoy the same social protection.

ARTICLE 26. (1) Everyone has the right to education. Education shall be free, at least in the elementary and fundamental stages. Elementary education shall be compulsory. Technical and professional education shall be made generally available and higher education shall be equally accessible to all on the basis of merit.

(2) Education shall be directed to the full development of the human personality and to the strengthening of respect for human rights and fundamental freedoms. It shall promote under-

standing, tolerance and friendship among all nations, racial or religious groups, and shall further the activities of the United Nations for the maintenance of peace.

(3) Parents have a prior right to choose the kind of education that shall be given to their children.

ARTICLE 27. (1) Everyone has the right freely to participate in the cultural life of the community, to enjoy the arts and to share in scientific advancement and its benefits.

(2) Everyone has the right to the protection of the moral and material interests resulting from any scientific, literary or artistic production of which he is the author.

ARTICLE 28. Everyone is entitled to a social and international order in which the rights and freedoms set forth in this Declaration can be fully realised.

ARTICLE 29. (1) Everyone has duties to the community in which alone the free and full development of his personality is possible.

(2) In the exercise of his rights and freedoms, everyone shall be subject only to such limitations as are determined by law solely for the purpose of securing due recognition and respect for the rights and freedoms of others and of meeting the just requirements of morality, public order and the general welfare in a democratic society.

(3) These rights and freedoms may in no case be exercised contrary to the purposes and principles of the United Nations.

ARTICLE 30. Nothing in this Declaration may be interpreted as implying for any State, group or person any right to engage in any activity or to perform any act aimed at the destruction of any of the rights and freedoms set forth herein.

E

BIBLIOGRAPHY

Aquinas, St. Thomas. *Summa Theologica,* in Hall, which see.

Aristotle. *Ethics,* in Hall, which see.

Black, Charles L., Jr. *The People and the Court* (The Macmillan Co., 1961).

Black, Hugo L. *"The Bill of Rights"* in *New York University Law Review* (April 1960).

Brant, Irving. *James Madison, Father of the Constitution* (Bobbs-Merrill Co., 1950).

Cardozo, Benjamin N. *The Growth of the Law* (Yale University Press, 1924).

——*The Nature of the Judicial Process* (Yale University Press, 1921).

Chafee, Zechariah. *Free Speech in the United States* (Harvard University Press, 1946).

Cheyney, Edward P. "Freedom and Restraint: A Short History" in *The Annals* (American Academy of Political and Social Science, November 1938).

Cicero. *De Legibus,* in Hall, which see.

——*De Republica,* in Hall, which see.

Corwin, Edward S. *The "Higher Law" Background of American Constitutional Law* in *Harvard Law Review* (1928–1929) and republished with prefatory and biographical notes by Clinton Rossiter (Cornell University Press, 1955).

Cushman, Robert E. *Civil Liberties in the United States* (Cornell University Press, 1956).

Douglas, William O. *A Living Bill of Rights* (Doubleday & Co., 1961).

——*The Right of the People* (Doubleday & Co., 1958).

Federalist, The. With introduction by Edward Mead Earle (Modern Library, 1941).

Greenberg, Jack. *Race Relations and American Law* (Columbia University Press, 1959).

Griswold, Erwin N. *The Fifth Amendment Today* (Harvard University Press, 1955).

Hall, Jerome, ed. *Readings in Jurisprudence* (Bobbs-Merrill Co., 1938).

Hand, Learned. *The Bill of Rights* (Harvard University Press, 1958).

Harper, Robert Francis, ed. *Hammurabi, King of Babylon* (University of Chicago Press, 1904).

Hobbes, Thomas. *Leviathan,* ed. Michael Oakeshott (The Macmillan Co., 1947).

Jackson, Robert H. *The Supreme Court in the American System of Government* (Harvard University Press, 1955).

Jefferson, Thomas (see Padover).

Konvitz, Milton R. *The Constitution and Civil Rights* (Columbia University Press, 1947).

Konvitz, Milton R., and Clinton Rossiter, eds. *Aspects of Liberty* (Cornell University Press, 1947).

Locke, John. *Second Treatise of Civil Government,* in *Of Civil Government* (Everymans Library, 1924).

Meiklejohn, Alexander. *Political Freedom* (Harper & Bros., 1960).

Miller, Merle. *The Judges and the Judged* (Doubleday & Co., 1952).

Padover, Saul K., ed. *Thomas Jefferson on Democracy* (New American Library, 1946).

Paine, Thomas. *Common Sense* (Dolphin Books, 1959).

Perry, Richard L., and John C. Cooper, eds. *Sources of Our Liberties* (American Bar Foundation, 1959).

Pfeffer, Leo. *Church, State, and Freedom* (Beacon Press, 1953).

Rogge, O. John. *The First and the Fifth* (Thomas Nelson & Sons, 1960).

Taylor, Telford. *Grand Inquest: The Story of Congressional Investigations* (Simon & Schuster, 1955).

Weinberger, Andrew D. "*A Reappraisal of the Constitutionality of Miscegenation Statutes*" in *Cornell Law Quarterly* (Winter 1957). Revised and republished in *Law Review Digest* (January–February 1957), *Revue de Droit International* (June 1957), *Revista de la Facultad de Derecho* (July–September 1957), *Journal of Negro Education* (Fall 1957), *Law Review of University of Sto. Tomás* (November–December 1957), and *Journal of the National Medical Association* (May 1959).

F

TABLE OF CASES

The principal page references to the text appear first and, therefore, may be out of numerical order. Italicized page numbers refer to abridgments.

G

INDEX